WILD
FLOWERS
OF SOUTH AFRICA

BRAAM VAN WYK

Published by Struik Nature
(an imprint of Penguin Random House (Pty) Ltd)
Reg. No. 1953/00041/07
Estuaries No. 4, Oxbow Crescent
Century Avenue, Century City, 7441
PO Box 1144, Cape Town, 8000 South Africa

Visit **www.randomstruik.co.za** and join the Struik Nature Club
for updates, news, events and special offers

First published in 2000 as *A Photographic Guide to Wild Flowers of South Africa*
Second reworked edition (*Pocket Guide: Wild Flowers of South Africa*) 2015

Copyright © in text, 2000, 2015: Braam van Wyk
Copyright © in photographs, 2000, 2015: Braam van Wyk,
unless otherwise indicated alongside image
Copyright © in line drawings, 2015: Daleen Roodt
Copyright © in maps, 2000, 2015: Penguin Random House (Pty) Ltd
Copyright © in published edition, 2000, 2015: Penguin Random House (Pty) Ltd

Publisher: Pippa Parker
Managing editor: Helen de Villiers
Editors: Emily Bowles
Design director: Janice Evans
Designers: Gillian Black, Deirdre Geldenhuys
Cartographer: Genene Hart

Reproduction by Hirt and Carter Cape (Pty) Ltd
Printed and bound by Times Offset (M) Sdn Bhd, Malaysia

Print 978 1 77584 166 1
E-PUB 978 1 77584 351 1
E-PDF 978 1 77584 352 8

Front cover: Flame lily, *Gloriosa superba* (Braam van Wyk)
Back cover: Beetle daisy, *Gorteria diffusa* (Braam van Wyk); Cape everlasting, *Syncarpha vestita* (Braam van Wyk); common agapanthus, *Agapanthus praecox* (Braam van Wyk); pink sour fig, *Carpobrotus acinaciformis* (Braam van Wyk)
Title page: *Protea cynaroides*, the king sugarbush, floral emblem of South Africa (Braam van Wyk). The 'flower' is in fact a flower head composed of numerous white flowers, surrounded by showy, usually pink to red bracts. About 85 species of *Protea* (sugarbushes) occur in South Africa; all are woody plants, and most of the more conspicuous ones are shrubs or small trees (not the focus of this book).
Contents page: Common gazania, *Gazania krebsiana* (Braam van Wyk)

ACKNOWLEDGEMENTS

My thanks to all those who made it possible for this book to be produced, especially those
who contributed photographs. Many thanks to Daleen Roodt who prepared the line drawings
used in the glossary. My appreciation to Martie Dednam, Elsa van Wyk, Elizabeth Retief and
Elsa Pooley, who assisted in various ways with the preparation of the manuscript. The South
African National Biodiversity Institute is thanked for the use of plant distribution data. Many
thanks to the team at Struik Nature for their patience and support.

CONTENTS

The Cape, smallest of the world's six floristic kingdoms, is more or less congruent with the Fynbos Biome (see map opposite). The flowering shrubs in this picture are pincushions, Leucospermum cordifolium.

INTRODUCTION

For a country of its size South Africa's floristic and vegetational diversity is without equal in the world; over 22,000 plant species are native to the region. Many South African plants are strikingly beautiful, and several garden ornamentals that have become universally popular are derived from species native to the region. The principal objective of this book is to give the reader a glimpse of the region's floral riches. Common and conspicuous plant species that are likely to be seen, especially along the roadside, have been featured in this book. The species presented represent all the major vegetation types and include several weedy alien species that are naturalised in the region. Though this book covers many flowering plant species, inhabiting a range of vegetation types, it describes only a fraction of the species found in South Africa. Those who want more information on our flora are referred to related books on the topic, some of which are listed under 'Further reading' (see page 144).

South Africa has two distinct floristic kingdoms and is one of only a few countries in the world where one can drive overland from one kingdom to another; it certainly is the one where the change in species composition is most noticeable and the transition between two kingdoms most striking. South Africa is also the only country in the world to harbour an entire floristic kingdom, namely, the Cape Floristic Kingdom. The smallest kingdom by far, the Cape Floristic Kingdom has more than 8,000 plant species, at least 70% of which are strictly confined to the region. Groups that contribute extensively to the floristic diversity of the Cape are the ericas (730 species) and especially the families Proteaceae (proteas), Restionaceae (reeds), Iridaceae (irises), Asteraceae (daisies), Rutaceae (buchus), Fabaceae (legumes) and Mesembryanthemaceae (vygies). No fewer than eight plant families are more or less strictly confined to the Cape.

Outside the Cape, the flora of South Africa has a very different composition and is classified as part of the Palaeotropical Kingdom, a large floristic region that includes most of Africa, Madagascar, India, Malaysia and Indonesia. Prominent groups within this region are from families such as Poaceae (grasses), Mimosaceae (acacia family), Combretaceae (bush willow family), Convolvulaceae (morning glory family), Acanthaceae (acanthus family), Malvaceae (hibiscus family) and many others, mostly with a tropical affinity.

BIOMES

Vegetation can be described as the general effect produced by the growth forms of some or all the plant species in combination. World-wide the principal vegetation types are forest, savanna, thicket, grassland, semidesert, desert and fynbos (sclerophyllous shrubland). Development of these broad groupings, which represent different habitats, is determined by prevailing climatic conditions over large areas. It is mainly the structural features of a vegetation type that determine its associated macrofauna (e.g. birds, mammals).

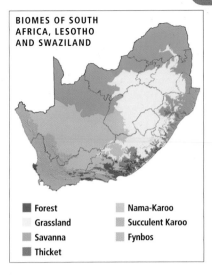

BIOMES OF SOUTH AFRICA, LESOTHO AND SWAZILAND

- Forest
- Grassland
- Savanna
- Thicket
- Nama-Karoo
- Succulent Karoo
- Fynbos

Areas relatively uniformly covered by any one of these broad vegetation types usually represent major biotic zones called biomes. Although biomes are not determined floristically, they do contain characteristic plant species adapted to the specific prevailing habitat conditions. South Africa has seven biomes (see map), which are briefly described below. By also considering floristic differences, the biomes are further divided into about 400 different vegetation types.

Forest Biome

Dominated by woody vegetation, a forest is multilayered with a continuous canopy cover. South Africa is very poorly endowed with forest; it is by far the smallest biome, covering less than 0.25% of the region. Forests usually occur as small isolated patches (rarely larger than 1km²) in relatively frost-free areas with a mean annual rainfall of usually more than 725mm. South Africa's forest can be broadly divided into three main types: Afromontane, Coastal and Sand Forest. These forests are rather poor in wild flowers, with many of the more colourful species occurring as shrublets or creepers along forest margins. Among the more conspicuous flowers on the shady forest floor are species of *Clivia*, *Dietes*, *Plectranthus* and *Streptocarpus*. A few epiphytic orchids, usually with white flowers, occur in the tree canopies.

Forest is relatively poor in wild flowers.

A flowering poison bulb, Boophane disticha (page 73), in grassland.

Grassland Biome

Grassland is found chiefly on the eastern half of the high central plateau of South Africa and the inland regions of KwaZulu-Natal and the Eastern Cape. These are summer-rainfall regions. Frost, fire and grazing maintain the grass dominance and prevent the establishment of trees. Although dominated by a single layer of perennial grasses, the majority of plant species in this biome are non-grassy herbs, most of which are perennial plants that sprout annually from large underground storage structures. Among the more showy plants are the so-called pre-rain flowers. These appear in spring before the first rains, especially following veld fires. Unfortunately, commercial afforestation and ploughing have already destroyed large parts of the biome.

Savanna Biome

Savanna covers about one-third of South Africa and is the largest biome in the region. It is confined to areas with summer rainfall and an often subtropical climate. The vegetation is characterised by a grassy ground layer with varying densities of emergent trees. Where the trees are tall and dense, the vegetation is often referred to as woodland. A more open parkland with smaller trees and shrubs is locally known as bushveld. Fire is an important natural factor, the suppression of which may result in bush encroachment, perhaps the biggest environmental problem in the biome at present. The wild flowers of this region are usually perennials, with annuals becoming more prominent in arid types of savanna, such as mopane bushveld.

The yellow flowers of devil's thorn, Tribulus zeyheri light up a patch of mopane bushveld (savanna).

Thicket Biome

Thicket is characterised by dense, deciduous or evergreen shrubs, with a few trees rising above, and lacks a conspicuous grass cover. Constituent plants are often spiny and/or thorny. It is sometimes classified under the Savanna Biome. Some of its variations are referred to as valley bushveld. This biome has a fragmented distribution and is mainly confined to hot arid river valleys in subtropical regions along the east coast; it is most extensive in the southern parts of the Eastern Cape. Wild flowers are conspicuous, many being perennial climbers or scramblers, whereas succulents and bulbous plants are common in the undergrowth.

Nama-Karoo Biome

This is the second largest biome in the region. It occupies the semidesert summer-rainfall region on the central plateau of the western half of South Africa, known as the Karoo. The vegetation is dominated by perennial woody shrublets (locally known as *bossies*), interspersed with scattered grasses and other forbs. This is often referred to as karroid vegetation. Many of the shrublets are quite attractive when in full flower, but mass flowering events are erratic and in response to good rains, which may be separated by years of drought.

Succulent Karoo Biome

A semidesert biome confined to areas with a low winter rainfall and extreme summer drought. The vegetation is dominated by dwarf perennial shrublets, many of which are leaf succulents. It is also referred to as karroid vegetation or, on the sandy coastal plains along the west coast, as strandveld. Floristically the second richest biome after fynbos, it is the centre of diversity for the vygies (Mesembryanthemaceae or Aizoaceae) and is rich in geophytes and annuals. Following good rains, annuals often create brightly coloured mass flowering displays on degraded or fallow lands, and are a major tourist attraction.

The Succulent Karoo Biome; the ground is covered by a pink vygie, Drosanthemum floribundum.

Fynbos Biome

Fynbos, Afrikaans for 'fine-leaved bush', refers to a vegetation type dominated by evergreen woody shrubs and shrublets with small, tough and often linear needle-shaped leaves. Also known as sclerophyllous shrubland, this vegetation type is characteristic of regions with a mediterranean-type climate (winter rain and summer drought). Based on floristic composition, two main vegetation groupings occur in this biome, namely renosterveld on nutrient-rich clayey soils and fynbos (not to be confused with the Fynbos Biome) on nutrient-poor sandy soils. The Cape Floristic Kingdom is fairly congruent with the Fynbos Biome, which has over one-third of all the plant species in South Africa; it is the only one of the world's six floristic kingdoms comprising only a single broad vegetation type. This region is world-famous for its floristic

Here, Gladiolus bonaspei *flowers in fynbos after a fire.*

diversity and abundance of showy wild flowers, notably Proteaceae, Ericaceae, Asteraceae and Iridaceae.

HOW TO USE THIS BOOK

This book covers South Africa, Lesotho and Swaziland ('the region'). Species have been grouped into six main colour sections, based on the general colour impression of the flower (or what the layman may take as the flower). Within each colour section, both the families and the species within them are arranged in alphabetical sequence.

1 **NAME:** Each species entry starts with the accepted scientific name, family name and an English and Afrikaans common name. In a few cases the scientific name is followed by recent synonyms in brackets. **An asterisk* indicates an alien species.**

2 **FLOWERING SEASON:** Peak flowering time is given in the form of seasonal indicators: spring = August–November; summer = November–March; autumn = March–May; winter = May–August.

3 **DESCRIPTION:** Descriptive text for each species is restricted to brief comments on habit, habitat and some of the plant's more obvious morphological features. This is followed by notes on aspects of behaviour, interactions with other organisms, importance to man, classification and references to related species.

4 **MAP:** Range-style distribution maps are provided for each species. Green shaded areas on the map serve as a rough guide to the core distribution area of a particular species.

5 **PHOTOGRAPH:** Each species description has a colour photograph of the flowers (in a few cases also the fruit).

Technical terms are explained in the glossary (page 140), or in the line drawings on pages 142 and 143.

Senecio venosus

E Highveld senecio **A** Hoëveldse senecio

Asteraceae
Spring

Erect perennial herb, up to 1m high, with a woody rootstock; occurring in grassland and bushveld, often in rocky places. Leaves stalkless, lanceolate to oblong-lanceolate, up to 120 × 30mm, blue-green, hairless, except for wool hidden deep in leaf axils; base heart-shaped; venation very conspicuous (translucent) when leaf is held up to the light. Flower heads (see page 142) numerous, in a spreading cluster at the end of a generally solitary, unbranched flowering stem, radiate or discoid; ray florets 5–7, yellow; disc florets yellow; involucral bracts ± eight, broad and flat.

A very common species in Highveld grassland. Apparently not as acutely toxic to livestock as some of the other members of the genus. Powdered root used in traditional

---

Vernonia fastigiata

E Narrow-leaved vernonia **A** Smalblaarbitterbossie

Asteraceae
Spring–Summer

Annual or short-lived perennial herb, which is usually much-branched and twiggy; occurring mainly in bushveld and associated grassland, often as a weed in disturbed places, particularly along roadsides. Leaves sparsely present, stalkless, ± 40 × 4mm; margin smooth. Flower heads (see page 142) produced at tips of stems, ± 20mm in diameter, purple, consisting of disc florets only; bracts long, bristle-tipped, recurved and woolly.

Plants are extended bloomers and flower heads are produced virtually throughout the growing season. The flower heads are extremely popular among a great variety of butterflies, and the presence of the plants can be recognised at a distance from the mere aggregation of these insects. In *V. poskeana* (= *Polydora poskeana*) the involucral bracts are usually neither spreading nor recurved.

Asteraceae
Winter–Spring

*Echium plantagineum

E Purple bugloss **A** Pers-echium

Boraginaceae
Spring

Annual or biennial herb, with one to many flowering stems, up to 0.8m high, most parts with soft, appressed hairs; occurring along roadsides, in waste ground and as a weed of cultivation. Basal leaves ovate to oblanceolate; side veins prominent above and below. Upper stem leaves stalkless; base heart-shaped. Flowers broadly funnel-shaped, blue or deep purplish blue; stamens five, of which two protrude.

A native of western Europe, southwestern Britain and the Mediterranean region. Rather similar to *E. vulgare*, a native of Europe, which is also naturalised in the region. The latter occurs mainly along the southern and central Drakensberg. Its basal leaves are narrowly lanceolate, the side veins are not prominent, and the stem leaves have tapering bases; flowers with four stamens protruding.

Haemanthus albiflos
🇪 White paintbrush 🇦 Witpoeierkwas

Amaryllidaceae
Autumn–Winter

Evergreen, clump-forming perennial, up to 400mm high, with a bulb; occurring in forest and thicket, usually in coastal areas. Leaves 2–4, strap-shaped, smooth or hairy. Flowers in a dense umbel (or 'brush'), ± 30mm long, surrounded by green bracts; perianth white; anthers yellow. Fruit a berry, oval, red when ripe.

Bulbs located just below or even partly above soil surface. Some forms have leaves with white spots. Bulb used for medicinal and magical purposes. Both leaves and bulbs have been shown to be effective against certain viruses. *H. pauculifolius*, a rare species from Mpumalanga and northwestern KwaZulu-Natal, has mostly a single leaf, longer umbels (up to 55mm), and flowers with the perianth lobes more spreading.

Aponogeton distachyos
🇪 Cape pondweed 🇦 Waterblommetjie

Aponogetonaceae
Winter–Spring

Perennial aquatic herb, with a tuber; occurring in dams, rivers and ditches. Leaves floating, lanceolate to oblong, 60–200 × 20–70mm, with a long stalk. Flowers in forked spikes, arranged in two rows on the upper surface, white, sweetly scented. Each flower subtended by a large bract-like petal.

Confined to the winter-rainfall area; plants survive as tubers when water dries up. Flowering spikes edible during various stages of development; when in bud, with open flowers, or with young fruit, the older spikes being firmer and less watery. The plant is cultivated commercially; flowers marketed fresh or canned. They are cooked with mutton to produce a delicious stew known as *waterblommetjiebredie*. Also used in salads and soups. The tubers, which are rich in starch, are also edible.

Zantedeschia aethiopica
🇪 White arum lily 🇦 Witvarkoor

Deciduous or evergreen perennial, up to 1.5m high, with a rhizomatous tuber; occurring in fynbos, grassland, bushveld and along forest margins, usually in wet places. Leaves broadly ovate-cordate, usually unspotted. Male and female flowers without petals or sepals borne on a yellow spadix, 50–75mm long, which is subtended by a large funnel-shaped spathe that is white inside, without a purple blotch at base (see arrow-leaved arum). Female flowers at base of spadix interspersed by sterile stamens.

A popular garden plant; extensively grown as a cut flower, especially in New Zealand, with many cultivars (also known as calla lilies). Leaves cooked as a pot herb in times of famine. Tubers formerly boiled and fed to pigs. Leaves and tubers used in traditional medicine.

Zantedeschia albomaculata
🇪 Arrow-leaved arum 🇦 Witvlekvarkoor

Deciduous perennial, up to 700mm high, with a discoid tuber; occurring in grassland, bushveld and along forest margins, usually in marshy places. Leaves ± arrow-shaped, with or without white spots. Male and female flowers without petals or sepals borne on a yellow spadix, which is subtended by a large, cylindrical spathe varying in colour: white, cream or pale yellow inside, usually with a dark purple blotch at base. Female flowers at base of spadix not interspersed by sterile stamens.

Used in traditional medicine.
Zantedeschia, a genus of eight species, is largely confined to southern Africa. Plants contain abundant needle-like crystals of calcium oxalate; chewing of raw material causes severe irritation of the mouth and throat.

OLAF WIRMINGHAUS

Arctotis venusta

E Free State daisy **A** Vrystaatse gousblom

Asteraceae

Spring–Summer

Greyish annual herb up to 600mm high; occurring in grassland and karroid vegetation, often in disturbed places such as fallow fields and along roadsides. Leaves crowded near base of plant, elliptic-obovate, with margin deeply toothed to pinnately dissected, greyish green, with white hairs. Flower heads (see page 142) on long, erect stalks, radiate, 70mm in diameter; ray florets with upper surface white or pale cream, coppery purple to mauve below; disc florets blue-black or purple.

A frost-hardy species often cultivated in gardens; sow seed in March for a floral display in spring. Generic name derived from the Greek *arktos* = a bear, and *Otis* = ear, perhaps alluding to the pappus scales on the fruit, the involucral bracts or the shaggy fruit. The specific name means 'beautiful'.

Callilepis laureola

E Ox-eye daisy **A** Wildemagriet

Asteraceae

Spring

Perennial herb, up to 600mm high, sprouting annually from a woody tuber; occurring in grassland. Leaves linear-lanceolate to lanceolate, ± 65 × 20mm, three-veined; margin smooth or toothed. Flower heads (see page 142) solitary at the ends of erect stalks, radiate, ± 60mm in diameter; ray florets white or creamy white; disc florets purplish black.

Flowering is stimulated by veld fires. Well known under the Zulu name *impila*, the tuber is extensively used in traditional medicine as a powerful remedy to treat numerous ailments. Use of the plant for these purposes should, however, be discouraged. The tuber is highly toxic, inducing both liver and renal necrosis, with often fatal results. *C. leptophylla*, which occurs mainly in Highveld grassland, has needle-like leaves.

Dimorphotheca pluvialis
E Cape rain daisy **A** Witbotterblom

Asteraceae
Winter–Spring

Annual herb, up to 300mm high, often branching from the base; occurring in strandveld, fynbos and karroid vegetation, often on sandy soils. Leaves alternate, strap-shaped, ± 70mm long; margin coarsely and bluntly toothed. Flower heads (see page 142) occur singly at the ends of erect stalks, up to 70mm in diameter, radiate; ray florets glistening white above, with a narrow purple band at the base, mauve below; disc florets purplish black or yellow.

Form brilliant patches in disturbed sandy areas in spring. Popular annual for mass planting in gardens, often combined with yellow and orange forms of *D. sinuata*. The violet ring around the centre varies in width, being much more noticeable in some cultivated forms. Plants may cause prussic acid poisoning in sheep.

Eriocephalus africanus
E Wild rosemary **A** Kapokbossie

Asteraceae
Winter–Spring

A greyish, much-branched perennial shrublet up to 1m high; occurring in karroid vegetation and strandveld. Leaves alternate or in tufts, needle-like or 3–5-lobed, ± 15mm long, greyish. Flower heads (see page 142) in dense clusters toward the ends of stems, radiate; ray florets petal-like, 2–5, white; disc florets reddish purple. Fruiting heads have a very conspicuous fluffy covering, resembling bits of cotton wool.

Leaves pleasantly aromatic; grazed by livestock, giving their milk a characteristic flavour. Fluffy heads once used to fill pillows. Formerly one of the favourite nest-building materials of the Cape Penduline-tit (a small bird), now also supplemented by wool from sheep. These remarkable nests have a false entrance that remains open; the true entrance can be closed.

Felicia muricata

E White felicia **A** Karooblommetjie

Asteraceae
Spring–Autumn

A bushy perennial herb with a woody base, up to 400mm high; occurring in grassland and karroid vegetation, proliferating in overgrazed places. Leaves in axillary tufts, narrowly strap-shaped, ± 15 × 1mm. Flower heads (see page 142) on leafless stalks at the tips of branches, radiate, ± 15mm in diameter; ray florets ± backward-pointing, white or mauve; disc florets yellow.

Ray florets tend to be mauve in karroid areas, white in grassland. They point backward at night and move upward during daylight. Palatable and well grazed by livestock. Used in traditional medicine; fresh material is crushed and the scent inhaled to relieve headaches. Also used to treat cows that are ill after calving. About 70 species of *Felicia* occur in the region, the majority with blue or mauve ray florets.

Metalasia densa

E Flowerbush **A** Blombos

Asteraceae
All year

A much-branched, rounded shrub or small tree, with erect branches; occurring in fynbos, strandveld and grassland, often along streams or among rocks. Branchlets white-felted. Leaves in tufts or scattered, stalkless, needle-like, somewhat twisted, often flexed downward, up to 15 × 2mm, sharp-tipped (hooked in *M. densa*), often with woolly white hairs; margin rolled downward. Flowers in branched terminal heads (see page 142), white, often tinged pink or purple, sweetly scented.

Plays a useful role in the stabilisation of coastal dunes. Leaves and twigs are brewed as a tea. Used in Lesotho, sometimes with other plants, as a fumigant during illness or after a death. Despite the hard spiny leaves it is eaten by sheep. Utilised as a fuel in areas where wood is scarce. More than 50 species of *Metalasia* are native to the region.

Osmitopsis asteriscoides

E Swamp daisy **A** Belsbos

Asteraceae
All year

A slender, sparsely branched perennial shrublet, up to 2m high, lower parts of stems leafless; occurring in fynbos, usually as dense stands in swampy places. Leaves stalkless, lanceolate, up to 80 × 18 mm, velvety and somewhat sticky because of glandular hairs. Flower heads (see page 142) radiate, up to 35mm in diameter, clustered on short side branches near the tips of main stems; ray florets white; disc florets yellow.

Crushed leaves with strong camphor smell, due to a volatile oil rich in camphor and eucalyptol. Traditional Cape-Dutch remedy for a variety of ailments, including chest complaints, stomach problems, inflammation, body pains, paralysis, cuts, swellings, fever and influenza; usually administered in the form of a brandy tincture (*belsbrandewyn*) or as a poultice of the dried herb.

Syncarpha vestita

E Cape everlasting **A** Kaapse sewejaartjie

Asteraceae
Summer

A robust, woolly perennial shrublet, up to 1m high; occurring in fynbos, usually in sandy soils derived from sandstone. Leaves closely arranged, narrow, greyish green, soft, thickly covered with white felt. Flower heads (see page 142) borne singly on erect stalks, ± 50mm in diameter, silvery white, with a purple or maroon centre.

Flower heads are very attractive, even when still in bud. Extensively collected for use in dried-flower arrangements; scarce in some areas due to over-picking. Flower heads of *Helichrysum* are very similar to those of *Syncarpha* and *Edmondia* (both confined mainly to the Western Cape). A useful field character is that the leaf margins in the latter two genera are often rolled upward, at least toward the tip, but this is not very clear in *S. vestita*.

Rhigozum trichotomum
E Threethorn **A** Driedoring

Bignoniaceae
Spring–Summer

A rigid, woody shrublet, up to 2m high, spreading by means of underground stems; occurring in karroid vegetation, usually in sandy soils. Stems tend to branch in threes, hence the specific name *trichotomum* (Greek) = divided into three. Leaves clustered on short shoots, narrowly egg-shaped, up to 12 × 3mm, blue-green. Flowers solitary on short shoots, ± stalkless; corolla with a broad tube and five spreading lobes, white to pale cream or reddish. Capsule spindle-shaped, up to 100 × 3mm; seed with transparent wings.

Unpalatable to livestock, although flowers and capsules are browsed. Plants proliferate in overgrazed veld, often forming impenetrable thickets; covers thousands of hectares in the northern parts of the Great Karoo and adjacent Kalahari.

PIET VAN WYK – AGFA

Heliotropium nelsonii (= *H. steudneri* of some authors)
E Common heliotrope **A** Hamelstertjie

Boraginaceae
Spring–Autumn

An erect, perennial shrublet, up to 800mm high; occurring in bushveld and grassland, often in disturbed places. Leaves with short stalks, alternate, simple, lanceolate; margin wavy. Flowers in simple or forked terminal spikes, the latter ± coiled downward at the tips, with flowers pointing upward; corolla of five fused petals, ± 5mm in diameter, lobes oblong, with ± rounded or broadly tapering tips, white with a yellow throat.

About 15 species of *Heliotropium* are native to the region. They usually have white flowers in markedly curled, one-sided spikes. *H. ciliatum*, a common species along roadsides, has corolla lobes with hair-like tips. Generic name from the Greek *helios* = the sun and *trope* = to turn, referring to the old belief that the spikes turned with the sun.

Berzelia lanuginosa
🇪 Marsh buttonbush 🇦 Vleiknoppiesbos

Evergreen, erect, much-branched perennial shrub, up to 2m high; occurring in fynbos, usually in dense stands along watercourses or in marshy places. Branches tend to droop. Leaves ± 0.5mm wide, needle-like, spreading. Flowers very small, massed together in many rounded heads on branched terminal stems; heads ± 8mm in diameter; stamens conspicuously elongated, white to pale cream, giving a fluffy appearance to the heads.

Presence of the plants is a good indicator of permanent water. Also known in Afrikaans as *kolkol*, because the localised stands of plants stand out, especially when in flower, as distinct patches (Afrikaans = *kolle*) against the uniform green of the surrounding fynbos. Flower heads with stalks often swollen and bright red in *B. abrotanoides*. The genus comprises 12 species.

Brunia noduliflora
🇪 Common snowbush 🇦 Gewone stompie

Evergreen perennial shrublet, up to 1m high, with a woody rootstock; occurring in fynbos, usually on mountain slopes. Leaves scale-like, up to 3mm long, closely packed, pressed against the stem. Flowers very small, clustered into dense, rounded heads, ± 10mm in diameter; heads surrounded at the base by tightly packed, hairy bracts; stamens elongated and giving a fluffy appearance to the heads, white or pale cream; styles two per flower. Fruiting heads greyish, may remain on plants for a year or more.

Resprouts after veld fires. Very similar in appearance to *Berzelia*, which has flowers with a single style. With the exception of one very rare species in Pondoland, the Bruniaceae (12 genera and about 80 species) are all confined to the Cape Floristic Kingdom.

Scabiosa columbaria

E Wild scabious **A** Jonkmansknoop

Dipsacaceae
Spring–Summer

Slender perennial herb, up to 1m high, with a woody rootstock; occurring in fynbos, grassland and bushveld. Leaves mainly in a basal rosette, the latter spoon-shaped, margins varying from smooth to toothed or deeply lobed; stem leaves smaller, often deeply lobed once or twice. Flowers in long-stalked, flat-topped terminal heads, 25–35mm in diameter; corolla downy, white, lilac to pink, peripheral ones larger, ± two-lipped; sepals bristly, persisting on the fruit.

Widespread from the Cape up to Ethiopia; also in Europe. The compact inflorescences achieve a much more conspicuous floral display than would scattered solitary flowers; visited by a great variety of pollinators, including bees, beetles, wasps and butterflies. Used in traditional medicine for a variety of ailments.

Albuca setosa (= *A. pachychlamys*)

E Small white albuca **A** Kleinwitslymstok

Hyacinthaceae
Spring

Erect, bulbous herb, up to 300mm high; bulb scales ending in persistent fibres; occurring in grassland and bushveld. Leaves produced after flowering, few, ± 300mm long, ± 20mm wide at base. Flowers in racemes, all facing upward; perianth with six lobes, outer three spreading, inner three converging and hooded at the tips, white, with broad green to greenish-brown central stripe on back; stamens concealed by the inner perianth lobes.

One of the typical pre-rain flowers of the Grassland Biome. Flowering is stimulated by veld fires; fruit matures exceedingly fast. Leaves and flower stalk rich in slime, hence the Afrikaans common name (*slym* = slime). About 60 species of *Albuca* occur in the region. Flowers mostly white or yellow, very similar-looking; species recognition often difficult.

Drimia altissima (= *Urginea altissima; U. epigea*)

E Tall white squill **A** Reuseslangkop

Hyacinthaceae
Spring

Slender, erect, deciduous perennial, up to 2.5m high with a large, thick-scaled bulb, the latter borne above or just below the ground; occurring in bushveld and thicket, usually in dense colonies. Leaves erect, 150–300 × 20–30mm, leathery, grey-green. Flowers in a raceme at the end of a sturdy, exceptionally long, erect stalk; tepals white, with a green or brownish streak down the middle.

Leaves produced after flowering. Flowers open early morning and close by midday. Bulbs used in traditional medicine to treat colds and backache and also for magical purposes. Whole plant highly toxic; active principles include cardiac glycosides, the cause of acute and often fatal poisoning in livestock. Cut bulb rubbed on inner surface of leather skins laid out to dry for tanning; deters dogs.

Dietes grandiflora

E Large wild iris **A** Grootwilde-iris

Iridaceae
Spring–Summer

Evergreen, clump-forming perennial, up to 1.5m high, with a sturdy, creeping rhizome; occurring in grassland and along forest margins, often in wet places. Leaves erect, sword-shaped, ± 1,000 × 15mm, dark green. Flowers large (up to 100mm in diameter), in clusters of three or four at the ends of irregularly branched, erect stalks; tepals six, white, outer three larger, with a yellow bearded blotch edged by brownish speckling at the base; style with three slightly spreading, leaf-like lobes, each two-fid, violet.

A popular garden plant. Although the flowers are fleeting, each one lasting only a day, new flowers open each day over an extended period of time. *D. iridioides* has flowers up to 60mm in diameter; occurs in shady places in forest, young plants often developing on old flowering stems.

Gladiolus longicollis

E Honey flower **A** Graspypie

Iridaceae
Spring–Summer

A slender, erect perennial, up to 800mm high, with a corm; occurring mainly in grassland. Leaves three, only the lowermost with a well-developed blade, ± 750 × 5mm, with four narrow, longitudinal grooves. Flowers 1–4 on long, slender, erect stem, opening one at a time; perianth with tube 50–110mm long, lobes triangular, creamy white inside, often mottled with brown, brownish-speckled on the outside.

Flowers open in the late afternoon, or during the day in cool, misty weather. In the evening they release a sweet, penetrating scent, reminiscent of carnations and cloves; pollinated by hawkmoths. Hawkmoth-pollinated flowers are generally pale in colour, with long nectar-filled floral tubes and a heavy scent in the evening and night, features clearly displayed by this species.

Ocimum obovatum (= *Becium obovatum*)

E Cat's whiskers **A** Katsnor

Lamiaceae
Spring–Summer

Low-growing, perennial shrublet, up to 300mm high, with erect, annual, herbaceous stems from a woody rootstock; occurring in grassland and bushveld. Leaves ± stalkless, 15–40 × 5–20mm, opposite, smooth to hairy. Flowers crowded at the ends of erect stalks; corolla two-lipped, 10–18mm long, white to pale mauve, upper lip usually with longitudinal violet lines (nectar guides), rarely pure white; stamens protruding for up to 20mm, curved upward.

Typical pre-rain flower of the Grassland Biome. Adapted to grassland that is periodically burned; flowers profusely after fire. Extrafloral nectaries on the inflorescence attract ants for protection. Crushed leaves have a delicate perfume. An infusion of the pounded root is used to treat stomach troubles; also reputed to be a hair-restorer. Larval food plants for several butterflies of the genus *Lepidochrysops*.

Salvia disermas (= S. rugosa)

E Limestone sage **A** Kalksalie

Lamiaceae
Summer

Perennial herb, up to 500mm high, with a woody rootstock; occurring in grassland and karroid vegetation, often on limestone. Leaves mainly crowded at base of plant, broadly ovate to oblong-lanceolate, rough and hairy above; venation distinctly raised below; margin irregularly scalloped or toothed. Flowers in whorls of ± six toward the ends of erect stalks; corolla two-lipped, 15–30mm long, white, pale blue or pale mauve.

Strongly aromatic when crushed; widely used in traditional medicine. Leaves and flowers used as a revitalising tea or to bring down fever. Leaves, often mixed with root of *Rubia horrida*, are also used to treat skin disorders. Tends to proliferate in overgrazed veld. Closely related to *S. radula*, the leaves of which are white and woolly below.

Lanaria lanata (= L. plumosa)

E Cape edelweiss **A** Kapokblom

Lanariaceae
Summer

Erect perennial, up to 800mm high, with a ± vertical rhizome; occurring in fynbos, especially on rocky mountain slopes on sandy soils derived from sandstone. Leaves in a tussock, tough, narrow, dull green, ± hairless, with ± nine prominent parallel veins. Flowers small, opening in succession, clustered in much-branched panicles at the end of a sturdy, erect stalk, the whole being densely covered by woolly white hairs; perianth with six lobes, densely hairy outside, mauve and hairless inside.

Blooms profusely after fire. Although the individual flowers are mauve, the inflorescence appears white from a distance. The only member of the family; endemic to the Cape Floristic Kingdom. Previously classified under Haemodoraceae. Scientific name from the Latin *lana* = wool.

*Lilium formosanum
E Formosa lily **A** Formosalelie

Liliaceae
Summer

Erect, single-stemmed perennial, up to 1.5m high, with a bulb; occurring as a weed in grassland, often along roadsides and in marshy places, especially along the northeastern Drakensberg Escarpment. Leaves arranged all along stem, strap-shaped, ± 180 × 10mm. Flowers in terminal racemes of 3–10, large (130–200mm long), slightly drooping; perianth funnel-shaped, white, each segment with a reddish keel.

A native of Taiwan (which was formerly known as Formosa). Flowers sweetly scented. *Lilium* (± 100 species) represents the true lilies, all of which are from the northern hemisphere; extensively cultivated with many hybrids. *L. candidum* (Madonna lily; Israel, Lebanon and Balkans) cultivated since at least 1,500 BC for its white flowers, which are used in scent-making; may be the Rose of Sharon of the Bible.

Mesembryanthemum guerichianum
E Ice plant **A** Brakslaai

Mesembryanthemaceae
Spring–Summer

Annual or short-lived perennial succulent with robust, creeping stems; occurring in fynbos, strandveld and karroid vegetation; often forming dense stands in seasonal streams, flood plains, brackish areas and disturbed places. Most parts covered in glistening, collapsible, round cells, specialised for water storage. Leaves large and conspicuous (lettuce-like), folded upward along the midrib, green, usually tinged red. Flowers in clusters at ends of stems; petals numerous, white, pale yellow or pink.

Flowers open in bright sunlight and close at night; pollinated by honeybees. Formerly a solution prepared from dried or fresh leaves was used to remove hair from skins during tanning. May cause oxalate poisoning in sheep and goats, although not readily grazed.

JOHN MANNING

Jasminum multipartitum
E Common wild jasmine **A** Gewone wildejasmyn

Oleaceae
Spring–Summer

Perennial, ± climbing shrub, up to 3m high; occurring in thicket and bushveld, often in rocky places. Leaves opposite, simple, ± hairless; stalk up to 5mm long, appearing articulated (with knee-like thickening) ± in the middle. Flowers solitary or in clusters at the ends of main and side twigs; corolla with ± 11 lobes, white above, brick red below; buds red. Fruit a twin berry, often only one half developing, shiny black when ripe.

Widely cultivated in gardens. Flowers heterostylous; all flowers on certain plants short-styled and on others long-styled. Fertilisation takes place only between flowers of different style length, thus ensuring outcrossing. They are sweetly scented and pollinated by hawkmoths. *J. stenolobum* (mainly Mpumalanga and Limpopo) has hairy leaves.

**Oenothera tetraptera*
E White evening primrose **A** Witaandblom

Onagraceae
Spring–Autumn

Low-growing perennial herb, with many stems from a woody taproot; covered with long hairs throughout; occurring as a weed in disturbed areas, often along roadsides. Leaves variously lobed and toothed, at least some in a basal rosette; margin often wavy. Flowers ± 60mm in diameter; petals four, at the end of a nectar-containing calyx tube, free, white fading to purplish pink.

A native of Texas and Mexico. Flowers open just before sunset and last only a single night; pollinated by hawkmoths. Mature flower buds can be induced to open before one's eyes if enclosed by both hands in late afternoon. All ± 130 species of *Oenothera* (evening primroses) are native to North and South America. About 15 species naturalised as weeds in South Africa.

Rogeria longiflora
E White flower **A** Witblom

Pedaliaceae
Summer–Autumn

Robust, erect annual herb, up to 2m high; occurring in semidesert areas, often along roadsides. Leaves opposite, stalked, ovate, up to 300mm long. Flowers in groups in axils of leaves; corolla tubular, with spreading lobes and a distinct basal spur, up to 80mm long, white streaked with pink. Capsules ovoid, large (40–60mm long), woody, with two spines toward base on dorsal side, dehiscent, many-seeded.

Leaves unpleasantly scented. Dry remains of plants, with ripe (brown) capsules, may persist for several months; especially noticeable along roadsides. Seed roasted, ground, mixed with fat and applied to wounds to stop bleeding and to relieve the pain from burns. Heated leaves are used as a poultice to heal cracked nipples in breastfeeding mothers.

HESTER STEYN

Anemone fanninii
E Giant wild anemone **A** Grootanemoon

Ranunculaceae
Spring–Summer

Robust perennial herb up to 1m high, sprouting annually from a woody rootstock; occurring in grassland, usually in moist or rocky places. Leaves stalked, in a basal rosette, palmately 5–7-lobed, 250–350mm in diameter, thick, hairy above and below; margin toothed, teeth often with reddish tips; stalk ± 700mm long. Flowers in clusters of two or three at the end of a tall, erect stalk, fragrant; sepals petaloid with indented tips, up to 70mm long, white, often tinged pink; stamens numerous, with yellow anthers.

Flowering is stimulated by veld fires; the new leaves mature after the plant has flowered. An infusion of the leaf is used as a purgative and to treat biliousness. Like many other grassland plants the giant wild anemone is difficult to grow in suburban gardens.

MARK ROBERTSON

Clematis brachiata

E Traveller's joy **A** Klimop

Ranunculaceae
Summer–Autumn

Herbaceous or ± woody perennial vine, climbing vigorously by means of twining leaf stalks; occurring in wooded grassland and bushveld, usually in rocky places. Leaves opposite, 3–5-foliolate. Flowers solitary in leaf axils or in branched inflorescences at ends of stems, produced in abundance, sweetly scented; petal-like sepals white to pale cream, densely covered with hairs pressed close to the blade; stamens numerous and showy. Fruits numerous with long, feathery, silvery white styles.

Very conspicuous along roadsides during autumn when fruiting plants form silvery white masses over woody vegetation. A tea made from the leaves is used to treat headaches, colds and chest ailments. Root and stem used as a remedy against syphilis and for a host of other ailments.

Walafrida saxatilis (= *Selago saxatilis*)

E White bitterbush **A** Witaarbos

Scrophulariaceae
Summer

Perennial shrublet, up to 400mm high with erect stems; occurring in karroid vegetation and grassland, often in deep, stony soils. Leaves in clusters, strap-shaped or ± needle-like, up to 4 × 0.8 mm; margin smooth. Flowers very small, in compact, 12–20mm-long panicles, each comprising many small spikes at the end of shoots; petals five, irregular, with two facing up and three down, white; stamens and style exserted.

Stem with its stiff, spreading leaves resembles a pipe cleaner. Unpalatable to livestock. Proliferates in deteriorating veld. Generic name commemorates Walafrid Strabo (809–849 AD), a medieval monk, also known as 'Walafrid the Squint-eyed', who wrote a book on gardening. About 170 species occur in the region; flowers white or mauve to blue.

BOSSIE KOTZÉ

Thunbergia atriplicifolia
E Natal primrose **A** Grasveld-thunbergia

Acanthaceae
Spring–Summer

Perennial shrublet, up to 400mm high with a tuberous rootstock and milky latex; occurring in grassland. Leaves ± stalkless, opposite, 20–60 × 10–35mm, ± densely covered with soft hairs throughout; base rounded or heart-shaped. Flowers axillary, with two large overlapping bracts clasping the base; corolla pale cream with the inside of the tube pale yellow; stamens four, with broad, flat filaments.

Plants flower profusely after veld fires. Various parts used in traditional medicine. A hairwash is prepared from the leaf or unripe fruit. Differs from several other cream-flowered species of *Thunbergia* in the region in that it is not a twiner or scrambler. About 11 species are native to South Africa; in the past sometimes placed in a separate family, Thunbergiaceae.

Gomphocarpus fruticosus (= *Asclepias fruticosa*)
E Milkweed **A** Melkbos

Asclepiadaceae
Spring–Summer

Evergreen perennial shrublet up to 1.5m high, with milky latex; occurring in grassland and bushveld, often in disturbed places. Leaves opposite, linear or linear-lanceolate. Flowers (see page 142) in axillary umbels, usually pendulous; corolla lobes reflexed, cream; corona with blunt tips, greenish. Fruit inflated, spindle-shaped, sparsely covered with bristle-like hairs.

Stems contain a strong, silky bark fibre, formerly used for sewing. Used in traditional medicine to treat chest and stomach problems. Milky latex reportedly effective in the removal of warts. Seed hairs formerly used as tinder and to stuff pillows and mattresses. Larval food plant of the African monarch butterfly (*Danaus chrysippus orientis*). Toxic substances derived from the plant are passed via pupa to adult insect offering protection against predators.

Bulbine latifolia

E Broad-leaved bulbine **A** Rooiwortel

Asphodelaceae

Spring

Succulent perennial, up to 1m high; aloe-like, but without thorns; occurring in karroid vegetation and valley bushveld (thicket). Leaves in a basal rosette, ± 300 × 80mm, thick and fleshy, dull green, the tapering tips often recurved (± wilted). Flowers in long racemes at the ends of erect, unbranched stalks, yellow, with bearded filaments. Fruit a capsule, globose, splitting open with three valves.

Sap used in traditional medicine to treat skin disorders (see next species), whereas an infusion or brandy tincture of the dried root is taken internally for a variety of ailments, including diabetes, rheumatism, urinary complaints and blood disorders. Very similar to *B. natalensis* (with which it may well be conspecific), a species extending from the Eastern Cape through KwaZulu-Natal to the Mpumalanga Escarpment.

Bulbine narcissifolia

E Strap-leaved bulbine **A** Wildekopieva

Asphodelaceae

Spring–Summer

Erect perennial herb, up to 300mm high, with a short rootstock and fleshy roots; occurring in grassland, often in large colonies. Leaves in a basal rosette, ± erect, flattened, 5–20mm wide, greyish green, ± fleshy. Flowers numerous, densely clustered at the end of a long, sturdy, erect stalk, yellow; filaments with long yellow hairs. Fruit a capsule, three-locular; many seeds per locule.

Plants may proliferate in overgrazed areas. The leaves contain a yellowish sap that is a popular traditional first-aid remedy. Sap is applied directly from a freshly broken leaf onto burns, sunburned skin, rashes, cold sores, insect bites and minor cuts and scrapes. Several other members of the genus, all easily recognised by their yellow flowers and bearded filaments, are used in a similar manner.

Bulbinella latifolia

Asphodelaceae

E Broad-leaved cat's tail **A** Breëblaarkatstert

Spring

Sturdy, erect perennial herb, up to 1m high, with a fibrous, erect rhizome; occurring in karroid vegetation and fynbos, often forming large stands in seasonally damp areas. Leaves tapering, channelled, up to 500 × 65mm. Flowers small (6–8mm in diameter), densely clustered in cylindrical racemes on tall inflorescence stalks, yellow (var. *latifolia*) or rarely orange (var. *doleritica*; which is confined to the Nieuwoudtville area). Fruit a capsule, three-locular; seeds one or two per locule.

May be confused with *B. nutans*, which has much narrower (± 10mm) leaves and broader (± 50mm) conical racemes. The genus has a widely disjunct distribution; 17 species in the winter-rainfall area of the region; six in New Zealand. Distinguished from similar-looking members of *Bulbine* by its hairless filaments in the flower.

JOHN MANNING

Kniphofia porphyrantha

Asphodelaceae

E Highveld red-hot poker **A** Hoëveldvuurpyl

Spring–Summer

Erect perennial herb, up to 1m high, with fibrous roots; occurring in grassland, usually in marshy places and in dense groups. Leaves basal, ± flat above, at first erect, later arching, yellow-green; margin smooth. Flowers crowded into dense, spike-like inflorescences borne well above the leaves, tubular and ± drooping, orange when in bud, lemon yellow when open.

Used in traditional medicine to treat female ailments. Easily confused with several other similar-looking species; more than 50 species of *Kniphofia* occur in the region. *K. ensifolia* is a robust Highveld species with a distribution mainly west of the Drakensberg Escarpment, extending to the Northern Cape and western Free State. Its open flowers are pale yellow or greenish white.

Berkheya onopordifolia

E Tumbleweed berkheya **A** Tolbosdisseldoring

Asteraceae
Summer

Bushy, short-lived perennial herb, up to 1m high; occurring mainly in grassland and karroid vegetation. Leaves stiff and leathery, oblong, deeply pinnately lobed, up to 300 × 80mm, green above, white-felted or with glandular hairs below; margin with coarse, triangular, spine-tipped teeth, interspersed with spines. Flower heads (see page 142) solitary or a few together at the ends of stems, radiate, up to 90mm in diameter, ray and disc florets yellow; involucral bracts ± 10mm wide, spine-tipped.

After the fruiting heads have matured, the above-ground part of the plant dries out, breaks loose from the root and rolls about in the wind, thus distributing the seeds; dried plants often seen piled-up against fences along roadsides. Used in traditional medicine to treat feverish illnesses.

Didelta spinosa

E Saladbush **A** Slaaibos

Asteraceae
Spring

Shrub or small, slender tree, up to 2.5m high; occurring in semidesert areas, often in stony places. Leaves stalkless, ovate to elliptic, up to 70 × 60mm, thick and ± succulent, usually hairless; apex often spine-tipped; margin usually with irregularly spaced, spine-tipped teeth. Flower heads (see page 142) solitary at ends of branches, radiate, ± 60mm in diameter; ray and disc florets yellow; involucral bracts with the five outer ones leaf-like and spreading, the inner ones narrow and toothed.

Heavily browsed by livestock, notably horses; taller plants often with a rounded crown above the browse line. Leaves used in salads, hence the common names. *D. carnosa*, a herbaceous shrublet from sandy areas along the west coast, has narrow leaves with the margins rolled under; leaves in some forms have white hairs.

Euryops abrotanifolius

E Mountain resinbush **A** Bergharpuisbos

Asteraceae
Autumn–Spring

Erect perennial shrublet, up to 1m high, single-stemmed or sparsely branched; occurring in fynbos, usually on sandy or rocky slopes. Leaves up to 90mm long, pinnately divided into segments ± 1.5mm wide, leathery. Flower heads (see page 142) on long, slender stalks, radiate, ± 50mm in diameter, bright yellow; involucral bracts in one row, united to form a smooth cup. Plants often appear as pioneers after veld fires.

A showy species often found on Table Mountain. More than 80 species of *Euryops* occur in the region, many with yellow flower heads on long, slender stalks above the foliage. Generic name derived from the Greek *eurys* = large and *ops* = eye, alluding to the showy flower heads. Several species grown in gardens. Plants need well-drained soil and full sun, and are tender to frost.

**Flaveria bidentis*

E Smelter's bush **A** Smeltersbossie

Asteraceae
All year

Erect, leafy annual herb, up to 1m high; occurring in bushveld, very common as a weed along roadsides and in disturbed places. Stems yellowish, hairless. Leaves opposite, with very short stalks, lanceolate to elliptic, up to 80 × 20mm, with ± three prominent parallel veins; stalks of each leaf pair ± joined around the stem; margin toothed. Flower heads discoid (see page 142), with few flowers, yellow, arranged in dense terminal and axillary groups; involucral bracts 2–4, closely arranged in a single whorl to form a cylindrical tube.

A native of tropical America. First recorded in South Africa in 1917. Probably introduced with fodder during the Anglo-Boer War or as an impurity in bird seed. Easily controlled without herbicide by shallow cultivation or soil tilling during the seedling stage.

Gazania krebsiana

E Common gazania **A** Gewone botterblom

Asteraceae
All year

Low-growing annual or perennial herb, with milky latex; occurring in various vegetation types. Leaves in a basal rosette, long and narrow, greenish above, white-felted below; margin smooth, toothed or deeply lobed. Flower heads (see page 142) solitary, stalked, radiate, 30–80mm in diameter; ray florets yellow, white, orange, red or shades of yellow and orange, often brownish at the base, with or without a whitish/black blotch; disc florets same colour as the outer portion of ray florets.

A wide-ranging and extremely variable species, best subdivided into a number of taxa. Flowering in some forms stimulated by fire. Used for medicinal and magical purposes. Many showy cultivars are grown in gardens. Unfortunately, not suited as cut flowers; heads open only in bright sunlight.

Helichrysum decorum

E Coastal yellow everlasting **A** Kusgeelsewejaartjie

Asteraceae
Summer–Autumn

Erect biennial or short-lived perennial herb, up to 1.3m high; occurring in grassland or open bushveld, usually in coastal areas. Leaves on stems oblong-lanceolate or elliptic-lanceolate, up to 80 × 30mm, upper surface cobwebbed, lower surface with woolly greyish-white hairs. Flower heads (see page 142) ± 30mm in diameter, bright yellow, arranged in large, flat-topped panicles at the ends of stems.

An attractive, though little-known, garden plant. A number of very similar-looking, yellow-flowered species of *Helichrysum* occur in the region. *H. setosum* has sticky green leaves, and flower heads solitary at the tips of long, leafy branchlets arranged in small, flat-topped groups near ends of stems. *H. cooperi* has the flower heads arranged in well-branched, horizontally spreading panicles.

Helichrysum nudifolium
E Hottentot's tea **A** Hottentotstee

Asteraceae
Summer

Erect perennial herb up to 1.3m high; occurring in grassland and fynbos, often in dense stands. Leaves crowded near the base, linear-lanceolate to ± elliptic, the larger ones up to 600 × 300mm, contracted to a stalk-like base, 3–7-veined, green and rough-textured above, woolly and white below. Flower heads (see page 142) ± 3mm in diameter, very many arranged in compact, ± flat-topped or rounded panicles at the ends of stems; involucral bracts in ± six rows, bluntly pointed, pale or lemon yellow.

A very common species in high-rainfall montane grassland. Leaves aromatic and used in traditional medicine to treat chest ailments, fevers, wounds and headaches. *H. coriaceum* has flower heads ± 5mm in diameter, with straw-coloured involucral bracts. Common in Highveld grassland.

Hirpicium bechuanense
E Botswana marigold **A** Botswanagousblom

Asteraceae
Summer

Annual or short-lived perennial herb, up to 400mm high; occurring in bushveld, often alongside roads and in disturbed places. Leaves strap-shaped, grey-green above, white-felted below; margin toothed, with long, bristly hairs toward base. Flowers (see page 142) solitary at ends of branches, radiate; ray florets yellow, with tips of petals three-toothed; disc florets yellow; involucral bracts in seven or eight rows, ± united into a cup-like base with short, stiff hairs.

Flowers open only in bright sunlight. Plants have proved experimentally to be toxic to sheep, with death occurring within two days. There are about eight species in the genus, all confined to southern and East Africa. They are readily distinguished from related groups by the involucral bracts and leaves, which are often covered by long, bristly hairs.

Nidorella hottentotica

Asteraceae
Autumn–Winter

E Hairy nidorella **A** Harige stinkkruid

Erect, sparsely branched annual or short-lived perennial herb, up to 1.5 m high; occurring in grassland and bushveld, often in disturbed places. Leaves strap-shaped, often ± undulating, densely covered with woolly white hairs. Flower heads (see page 142) essentially discoid (ray florets very small, two-lipped), arranged in ± flat-topped terminal groups, bright yellow.

Inflorescences are visited by a wide range of insects. *N. auriculata* is common in KwaZulu-Natal and along the Mpumalanga Escarpment. It has hairy (though not whitish) leaves, with the veins prominent below and the base ± eared. *N. resedifolia*, a widespread weedy annual, has roughly hairy leaves that are often ± pinnately lobed. It is particularly common in North West, especially on old cultivated lands.

Pentzia globosa

Asteraceae
Summer

E Grey karoo **A** Vaalkaroo

Rounded shrublet, up to 400mm high; occurring in karroid vegetation and in grassland. Leaves alternate or in clusters, grey-green, 4–6 × 0.1–0.3mm, three-fid or ± pinnately lobed. Flower heads (see page 142) borne near the tips of branches, stalked, discoid, ± 6mm in diameter, yellow.

One of the most abundant bushes in the eastern parts of the Karoo; fairly unpalatable to livestock and often proliferating in overgrazed areas. The related *P. incana*, one of the dominant bushes in the Karoo, is of considerable economic importance as it is readily grazed by sheep and forms an important part of their diet. It has shorter (2–3mm), undivided leaves. Also, some of the branches often curve downward and root, thus anchoring them to the ground. Aromatic leaves impart a distinctive flavour to Karoo mutton.

Senecio consanguineus
E Starvation senecio **A** Hongerbos-senecio

Asteraceae
Autumn–Spring

Bushy annual herb, up to 1m high, with a long taproot; most parts with sticky hairs; occurring in grassland, usually along watercourses and on rocky ridges, also very common as a weed on arable land. Leaves stalkless, strap-shaped, up to 50 × 20mm; base ± eared, stem-clasping; margin sharply and coarsely toothed. Flower heads (see page 142) radiate; ray florets usually 6–8, yellow, reflexed with age; disc florets yellow; involucral bracts in one row, sticky.

One of the few indigenous plant species that has become a troublesome weed; very conspicuous in maize fields during late winter, especially in North West. When fields are ploughed in late winter and spring, the abundantly produced fluffy seeds may block the radiators of tractors, hence its other name *radiatorbossie* (radiator bush).

Senecio inornatus
E Tall marsh senecio **A** Groot vlei-senecio

Asteraceae
Summer

Robust perennial herb, up to 2m high, with a woody rootstock; occurring in grassland, usually in marshy places. Basal leaves long (± 600 × 50mm) and elliptic, tapering to a long stalk at the base, often with traces of a woolly white covering; margin ± toothed. Flower heads (see page 142) clustered in ± flat-topped inflorescences at the ends of tall, erect, flowering stems, radiate; ray florets five, yellow, becoming reflexed at an early stage; disc florets yellow; involucral bracts ± 12. An easy-to-recognise species because of its tall flowering stems; often grows in dense stands.

Root decoctions used in traditional medicine to treat palpitations, phthisis, coughs and difficult breathing, but such treatment is potentially dangerous; plants contain highly toxic alkaloids that may cause liver damage.

Senecio latifolius

E Staggers bush **A** Dunsiektebossie

Asteraceae
Spring–Summer

Robust, bluish-green perennial herb, up to 1.5m high, with a woody rootstock; occurring in grassland and bushveld, often in dense colonies. Stems one or two, leafy throughout. Leaves elliptic, ± 90 × 40mm, leathery; base ± heart-shaped; margin ± widely toothed. Flower heads (see page 142) in flat-topped groups at the ends of stems, radiate; ray florets usually five, yellow; disc florets yellow.

Readily recognised by its unbranched stems, which are ± uniformly leafy. Plants tend to proliferate in disturbed areas. One of the species responsible for seneciosis, locally one of the most significant toxic reactions caused by poisonous plants in livestock. Chronic poisoning is known as 'Molteno straining disease' in cattle and *dunsiekte* in horses. Toxins affect the liver. Widely used in traditional medicine.

LORRAINE VAN HOOFF

Senecio pleistocephalus

E Bushveld canary creeper **A** Bosveldkanarieklimop

Asteraceae
Autumn–Winter

Robust, deciduous, succulent perennial creeper, usually clambering over woody vegetation; occurring in bushveld. Stems brittle. Leaves elliptic, glossy dark green, hairless; margin unevenly toothed. Flower heads (see page 142) in dense, flat-topped inflorescences, discoid; disc florets yellow, soon fading to brown; involucral bracts five.

A conspicuous plant in early winter when it brightens up the drab bushveld scenery; unfortunately the flowering period is very short. Flower heads are strongly honey-scented; very popular with honeybees and other insects. Various parts used in traditional medicine. Closely related to *S. brachypodus*, a succulent creeper from forest margins in the Eastern Cape and KwaZulu-Natal. It has pungently scented, radiate flower heads, with 5–8 involucral bracts.

Senecio polyanthemoides

E Forest margin senecio **A** Woudrand-senecio

Asteraceae

All year

Sparsely branched, bushy annual herb, up to 1.8m high; occurring along forest margins and in disturbed sites such as along roadsides, in old cultivated fields and felled plantations. Leaves lanceolate, up to 150 × 40mm, upper surface glossy, dark green and hairless, lower surface white-felted; margin rolled under, toothed. Flower heads (see page 142) in terminal panicles, radiate; ray florets ± eight, yellow; disc florets yellow.

Inflorescences visited by a wide range of insects. Introduced as a weed in the Cape Peninsula and Australia. Generic name based on the Latin *senex* = an old man; alluding to the fluffy white fruiting heads. One of the largest genera of flowering plants, comprising about 1,500 species, more than 300 reported from the region. Many are superficially very similar in appearance.

Senecio tamoides

E Canary creeper **A** Kanarieklimop

Asteraceae

Autumn–Winter

Robust, ± succulent perennial climber with twining stems; occurring along forest margins. Leaves ± triangular in outline, up to 80 × 80mm, light green and glossy, usually hairless; margin unequally lobed; stalk up to 80mm long. Flower heads (see page 142) in large, terminal clusters, radiate, up to 20mm in diameter; ray florets usually five, yellow; disc florets yellow; involucral bracts 6–8, ± 8mm long, swollen at the base.

A very showy species, widely cultivated as a climber in gardens. Plants must be supported by a trellis or allowed to twine into a tree. Stems root easily, but plants are sensitive to severe frost. They can be cut back after flowering, especially in cold areas where they tend to be semi-evergreen. Used in traditional medicine to treat certain human ailments and anthrax in cattle.

Senecio venosus

E Highveld senecio   **A** Hoëveldse senecio

Asteraceae
Spring

Erect perennial herb, up to 1m high, with a woody rootstock; occurring in grassland and bushveld, often in rocky places. Leaves stalkless, lanceolate to oblong-lanceolate, up to 120 × 30mm, blue-green, hairless, except for wool hidden deep in leaf axils; base heart-shaped; venation very conspicuous (translucent) when leaf is held up to the light. Flower heads (see page 142) numerous, in a spreading cluster at the end of a generally solitary, unbranched flowering stem, radiate or discoid; ray florets 5–7, yellow; disc florets yellow; involucral bracts ± eight, broad and flat.

A very common species in Highveld grassland. Apparently not as acutely toxic to livestock as some of the other members of the genus. Powdered root used in traditional medicine as a snuff for the relief of headaches.

BRAAM VAN WYK & SASA MALAN

Tripteris sinuata (= *Osteospermum sinuatum*)

E Karoo bietou   **A** Karoobietou

Asteraceae
Winter–Spring

Rounded, ± spreading perennial shrublet, up to 500mm high and 1m in diameter; occurring in karroid vegetation, often in large colonies. Leaves opposite, ovate to oblanceolate, 18–30 × 5–8mm, semisucculent, greyish green; margin widely toothed. Flower heads on short stalks at ends of stems, radiate, 25–35mm in diameter; ray and disc florets yellow; involucral bracts in a single row, with membranous margins and a sharp tip. Fruit with large wings, borne in drooping fruiting heads.

Plants are indicative of veld in good condition. Highly palatable to livestock; suitable for sowing into the veld to improve carrying capacity. Especially vulnerable to overgrazing during flowering and fruiting. Plants lose all or some of their leaves during unfavourable conditions.

JOHN MANNING

Rhigozum obovatum
E Yellowthorn **A** Geeldoring

Bignoniaceae

Spring

Rigid, compact shrub or small tree; occurring in karroid vegetation and valley bushveld, often in rocky places. Leaves opposite or in clusters, trifoliolate or simple, borne on short, spine-tipped side shoots; leaflets obovate, 5–13 × 2–5mm, greyish green; apex tapering. Flowers in axillary clusters, showy, bright yellow. Fruit a flattened pod-like capsule; seed with papery wings.

Leaves and pods are heavily browsed by game and livestock, particularly goats; highly resistant to drought. *R. brevispinosum*, with a more northerly distribution, has leaves that are predominantly simple; root used medicinally to treat oedema. *R. zambesiacum*, from low-elevation bushveld, has pinnately compound leaves with 3–5 pairs of leaflets. All these species are mass bloomers with showy yellow flowers.

**Raphanus raphanistrum*
E Wild radish **A** Ramenas

Brassicaceae

Winter–Summer

Erect annual or biennial herb, up to 800mm high; occurring as a weed on cultivated and fallow lands, also in other disturbed and often moist places. Basal leaves stalked, deeply pinnately lobed; stalk grooved. Flowers in axillary clusters; petals four, free, distinctly stalked, yellow or rarely white, sometimes with dark veins. Fruit pod-like, erect, narrowly tapering, at least four times as long as they are wide, constricted between the seeds, eventually breaking at constrictions into one-seeded portions.

A native of Europe, now a common weed, particularly in wheat fields in the Western Cape and eastern Free State. Seed poisonous, potentially dangerous when harvested with wheat used for bread or animal fodder, one of the clinical signs being diarrhoea. Widely used in traditional medicine.

Hermannia cuneifolia
E Yellow healing-bush **A** Geelpleisterbos

Byttneriaceae
Winter–spring

Spreading, much-branched, perennial shrublet, up to 1m high; occurring in karroid vegetation and fynbos. Leaves in tufts, wedge-shaped, 3–5 × 1–3mm, densely covered with star-shaped hairs on both surfaces; margin coarsely toothed. Flowers in spike-like groups at ends of shoots, drooping, sweetly scented; petals five, spirally twisted, 6–10mm long, yellow, fading to orange.

Once pollinated, the yellow flowers turn orange. This signals to pollinating insects which flowers still require their services. Palatable to livestock and drought resistant. Decoctions and infusions of the aromatic leaves are used in traditional medicine to treat sores; also taken internally for various ailments, hence the common names. Generic name after Paul Hermann (1640–1695), one of the first plant collectors at the Cape.

**Caesalpinia decapetala*
E Mauritius thorn **A** Kraaldoring

Caesalpiniaceae
Autumn–Spring

Robust, evergreen, scrambling shrub or climber; invading forest margins, roadsides, watercourses and disturbed places, often forming dense, impenetrable thickets. Branchlets with numerous, randomly scattered, straight to hooked thorns. Leaves bipinnately compound; leaflets up to 8mm wide. Flowers in elongated, erect, axillary racemes, pale yellow. Pods woody, flattened, sharply pointed at tip, indehiscent.

A native of Asia; cultivated for security hedging and ornament. It is a declared weed in South Africa. Generic name commemorates Andreas Caesalpino (1519–1603), an Italian botanist and physician, often called the first plant taxonomist. His book, *De Plantis* (1583), classified about 1,500 species on the basis of several vegetative and floral characters.

Chamaecrista mimosoides (= *Cassia mimosoides*) Caesalpiniaceae
E Fishbone cassia **A** Visgraat-cassia   Summer

Erect or prostrate annual or perennial herb, up to 500mm high; occurring in grassland and bushveld. Leaves stalked, pinnately compound, with a ± circular gland on the stalk below the basal pair of leaflets; leaflets 35–65 pairs, ± 8 × 2mm; axis with a long, narrow ridge along upper surface. Flowers in groups of 1–3 on internode above the leaf axil; petals yellow; sepals often tinged brownish or reddish. Pods dehiscent, splitting into two, spirally twisted valves.

As in most legumes, the leaflets fold closed at night. Used in traditional medicine to induce sleep, aid in the recall of dreams and treat various skin conditions, as well as dysentery and loss of appetite in children. The nine species of *Chamaecrista* in southern Africa have very similar flowers and are easily confused. Closely related to *Senna*, which has indehiscent pods.

Senna italica (= *Cassia italica*)   Caesalpiniaceae
E Wild senna **A** Elandsertjie   Spring–Summer

Perennial herb, with trailing stems from a woody black taproot; occurring in grassland and bushveld, often along roadsides. Leaves pinnately compound; leaflets 10–35 × 10–25mm, with rounded tips and small, finger-like glands in their axils. Flowers in stalked axillary racemes; petals bright yellow.

The sepals apparently secrete a nectary substance; they are actively visited by ants, the presence of which may protect the flowers against herbivorous insects. Seed used in traditional medicine and as a coffee substitute. Anthers have tiny apical pores; they must be vibrated at high frequency by bees to release the pollen. Forms are cultivated to provide some of the senna of commerce (dried leaflets and pods), a widely used purgative. Pods much favoured by eland, hence the Afrikaans common name.

Cleome angustifolia

Capparaceae

🇪 Yellow mouse-whiskers 🇦 Geel-cleome

Summer

Slender, erect, blue-green annual herb, up to 1.5m high; occurring in bushveld, often in mopane veld and along roadsides. Stems smooth, occasionally with spindle-shaped swellings. Leaves palmately compound, with 3–10 leaflets; stalk up to 60mm long. Flowers in lax, terminal racemes; petals four, free, yellow, usually with a violet blotch at the base, the two lateral ones larger, 9–24 × 5–12mm; stamens 8–18, the two or four fertile ones with filaments up to 40mm long, incurved. Fruit a pod-like capsule.

Following good rains, plants may appear in large numbers. About 20 species of *Cleome* occur in the region. They usually have spider-like pink or yellow flowers. In most of the region's other yellow-flowered species, all of the stamens are fertile. *C. gynandra*, with white flowers, is a popular leaf vegetable.

Commelina africana

Commelinaceae

🇪 Yellow commelina 🇦 Geeleendagsblom

Summer

Low-growing, hairless or hairy perennial herb with erect or trailing stems from a woody rootstock; occurring in grassland and bushveld, often on rocky outcrops. Leaves stalkless, long and narrow, flat or folded, forming a sheath at the base. Flowers borne in stalked, boat-shaped spathes; petals three, the upper two well-developed and stalked, the lower one reduced and ± colourless.

An extremely variable species; at least four varieties known in the region. Flowers open shortly after sunrise, fade before midday. Used in traditional medicine (especially the root) to treat various ailments, including venereal disease, sterility as well as heart and bladder complaints. Young shoots and leaves are cooked as a green vegetable; ground peanuts may be added as a condiment.

Merremia palmata

E Finger-leaved merremia **A** Vingerblaar-merremia

Convolvulaceae

Summer

Perennial herb, with long trailing or twining stems; hairless throughout; occurring in bushveld, often along roadsides. Leaves stalked, deeply palmately divided into 5–7 narrow (0.5–8mm), finger-like lobes, up to 60mm long. Flowers axillary, often solitary; corolla broadly funnel-shaped, 30–40mm in diameter, cream to pale yellow with a deep maroon 'eye'; anthers cream, ± spirally twisted. Fruit a capsule, ± globose, dehiscent.

The cream anthers are sharply contrasted against the dark corolla centre, undoubtedly a specialised adaptation to attract insect pollinators. *M. kentrocaulos*, a tall, ± woody climber with larger leaves (60–150mm long and wide) and flowers (50–70mm in diameter), is often seen along roads in the Kruger National Park and in Sekhukhuneland.

Kalanchoe thyrsiflora

E White lady **A** Geelplakkie

Crassulaceae

Autumn–Winter

Robust, erect succulent, up to 1.5m high, most parts covered with a powdery whitish covering; occurring on rocky ridges in grassland and bushveld. Leaves stalkless, 80–120 × 30–70mm, greyish green; margin smooth, often tinged with red. Flowers densely clustered toward the end of a tall, erect stem; corolla tube powdery whitish green outside, lobes spreading with upper surface deep yellow.

Leaves in a basal rosette for one or more years, gathering enough resources to flower. Following the formation of the tall inflorescence, which takes place in a single season, the particular rosette dies; new ones may sprout from the rootstock. Although poisonous, used in traditional medicine as treatment against intestinal worms; plants are known to cause paralysis in livestock.

Coccinia sessilifolia
E Sessile-leaved cucumber **A** Muisvoëlkomkommer

Cucurbitaceae
Summer

Blue-green, herbaceous perennial climber, with tendrils and a tuberous rootstock; occurring in grassland and bushveld. Leaves stalkless, deeply palmately five-lobed. Flowers axillary, male (illustrated) and female ones on separate plants; corolla pale cream to almost white, strongly veined. Fruit fleshy, pendulous, green mottled with white, ripening through yellow to red from the tip.

Both fruit and tuber used as food by the San people in the Kalahari; the former is best when gathered green and cooked as a vegetable, the latter is roasted or boiled. Seed dispersal facilitated by birds, the seeds being removed as the fruit ripens from the tip. Fruit-eating birds are strongly attracted to red fruit, especially those that sequentially ripen from yellow, through orange and red, to purple-black.

BRAAM VAN WYK & SASA MALAN

BRAAM VAN WYK & SASA MALAN

Aspalathus hirta
E Spiny-leaved aspalathus **A** Stekelblaar-aspalathus

Fabaceae
Spring

Erect, branched shrub, up to 2m high; occurring in fynbos and renosterveld. Stems short-haired to woolly. Leaves simple, needle-like, 5–12mm long, rigid, green, hairless or almost so, sharply spine-tipped. Flowers (see page 142) solitary or in pairs on short lateral shoots or branches, pea-like; petals bright yellow, the standard with short hairs on the back. Pods ± 10 × 4mm, densely woolly or silver-haired.

With about 280 species, *Aspalathus* is the largest genus of flowering plants strictly confined to South Africa, the majority of species being associated with the Cape Fold Mountains in the winter-rainfall area. *A. linearis* is the source of rooibos tea, an important commercial crop. Grown mainly in the Clanwilliam District, it contains no caffeine and is popular as a health beverage.

COLIN PATERSON-JONES

Calobota cytisoides (= *Lebeckia cytisoides*)

Fabaceae

🇪 Common whistle-bush 🇦 Gewone fluitjiesbos

Winter–Summer

Silvery, densely branched shrub, up to 2m high; occurring in fynbos and renosterveld, often in rocky places. Leaves usually trifoliolate; leaflets narrowly elliptic, with a powdery grey coating; stalk up to 30mm long. Flowers (see page 142) in short, loose racemes, pea-like, up to 20mm long, bright yellow. Pods cylindrical, ± 25 × 2mm.

Genus characterised by the lack of stipules and by young twigs remaining green for a long time due to delayed bark-formation; many members also with hairy petals. A strip of bark obtained from a related species can be pressed into a split reed to form a whistle (Afrikaans = *fluitjie*), hence the common names. *C. spinescens*, an important grazing bush from the central Karoo, is a twiggy, low-growing shrublet with spinescent branchlets and solitary flowers. It shows a preference for sandy soils, hence its common name, *sandganna*.

Crotalaria laburnifolia

Fabaceae

🇪 Bushveld crotalaria 🇦 Bosveld-crotalaria

Summer

Erect, sparsely branched annual herb, up to 600mm high; occurring in bushveld, often along roadsides. Leaves trifoliolate; leaflets ± elliptic, hairless; stalk 40–90mm long. Flowers (see page 142) in lax racemes, pea-like, yellow, often marked reddish brown. Pods inflated, often mottled with maroon when young.

Although the toxicity of this species is not known, crotalarias have been associated worldwide with poisoning in animals; the plants contain toxic alkaloids responsible mainly for severe liver and/or lung damage in livestock. Locally, members of the genus have been associated with *jaagsiekte*, a chronic respiratory disease in horses and mules, and *stywesiekte*, 'stiffsickness', in cattle, characterised by painful, warm hooves, and abnormal hoof growth during the chronic phase.

Cyclopia intermedia
🇪 Honeybush tea 🇦 Heuningbostee

Fabaceae
Winter–Spring

Evergreen, rounded perennial shrublet, up to 1m high; occurring in fynbos. Twigs golden brown. Leaves trifoliolate; leaflets elliptic. Flowers (see page 142) axillary, borne in clusters along the stems, pea-like, golden yellow, up to 15mm long, honey-scented. Pods flat, brown, many-seeded.

Resprouts after fire. Grown commercially. Leaves, twigs and flowers are cut into small pieces, allowed to ferment, dried, and used to make a tasty tea with a honey-like flavour, hence the common names. The tea, which is caffeine-free, can be reboiled to give several servings before the flavour is lost. A strongly brewed tea is used in traditional medicine to treat various ailments, including coughs, colds and bladder problems. *C. subternata* is an erect, sparsely branched shrub; regenerates from seed after fire.

BEN-ERIK VAN WYK

Eriosema psoraleoides
🇪 Shrubby yellow eriosema 🇦 Geelkeurtjie

Fabaceae
Summer

Silvery green perennial shrublet, up to 2m high; occurring in bushveld and grassland, often along roadsides. Branches strongly ribbed, with whitish hairs. Leaves trifoliolate, finely hairy above, densely silver haired below. Flowers (see page 142) in ± erect racemes of 10–50 flowers, pea-like, yellow. Pods compressed, ± 14 × 10mm, two-valved, hairy, dehiscent, two-seeded.

Flowers hang downward when in bud, rise to the horizontal plane as they open, and return to their former position when they close. As the standard petal becomes fully reflexed, this forces the wing petals to turn from the vertical into the horizontal plane, thus acting as a landing platform for pollinators. Ripe seeds are cooked as a vegetable. Leaf and root widely used throughout tropical Africa in traditional medicine.

Liparia splendens
E Mountain dahlia **A** Skaamblom

Fabaceae

All year

Spreading shrub, up to 2.5m high; occurring in fynbos, usually on rocky mountain slopes. Leaves simple, oval, sharply pointed, 30–50mm long, ± hairless, with three or more primary veins from the base of the blade. Flowers (see page 142) pea-like, arranged among prominent bracts in dense, drooping heads at the ends of curved branches; corolla with petals tightly overlapping, yellow flushed with orange. Pods compressed, two-valved.

The nodding flower heads have given rise to the Afrikaans common name (literally 'shy flower'). Adapted for pollination by sunbirds. While the bird is probing the flower for nectar, the tip of the keel petal dusts pollen onto its head, or picks up pollen left by another plant. *Liparia*, a genus of about 20 species, is confined to the Cape Floristic Kingdom.

Sebaea grandis
E Large-flowered sebaea **A** Grootblom-sebaea

Gentianaceae

Summer

Slender, erect annual herb, up to 350mm high; occurring in grassland, or in marshy places. Stems four-angled. Leaves opposite, stalkless, lanceolate, ± 40 × 15mm. Flowers terminal, solitary or few, ± 30mm in diameter; petals five, fused at the base, lobes spreading, pointed, cream or pale yellow; sepals with keel winged toward the base. Fruit a capsule, dehiscent, with many tiny seeds.

An infusion of the plant is used as a love charm emetic and has a pleasant, but bitter taste. About 45 species of *Sebaea* occur in the region. Most have cream or yellow flowers, 1–3 tiny glands on the anthers and a swelling somewhere along the style. The corolla lobes are twisted in bud and the calyx segments keeled or winged. Genus named after Albert Seba (1665–1736), a Dutch naturalist and author.

Sarcocaulon crassicaule (= *Monsonia crassicaulis*)

E Yellow bushman's candle   **A** Geelboesmanskers

Geraniaceae
Winter–summer

Fleshy, rigid, spiny, perennial shrublet, up to 500mm high; occurring in semidesert areas, usually in rocky places. Stems usually more than 10mm in diameter. Leaves long- and short-stalked, obovate, usually 15 × 9mm, with fine hairs; margin lobed, scalloped or toothed. Flowers solitary, axillary, up to 55mm in diameter; petals five, free, pale yellow.

Leaves produced only after good rains; stalks persistent, hardened into spines. Bark with a thick, ± translucent outer covering impregnated with wax; inflammable and burns with a smoky flame, even in green plants, hence the common names. Waxy bark very effective in preventing water loss; a plant of *S. patersonii* remained alive for 11 years unplanted after removal from the ground. The ± 20 species of *Sarcocaulon* are all confined to southern Africa.

Wachendorfia thyrsiflora

E Bloodroot   **A** Rooiknol

Haemodoraceae
Spring

Clump-forming perennial herb, up to 2m high, with stem-tubers; occurring in fynbos, usually in swampy places. Leaves basal, in erect fans, ± 800 × 80mm, conspicuously pleated along their length. Flowers in spike-like panicles at the ends of tall, erect stems; golden yellow.

Plants have a 'left- or right-handed' floral structure, a mechanism promoting cross-pollination. In 'left-handed' flowers the style along with one of the three stamens is deflected to the left; a reverse situation exists in 'right-handed' ones. Grown as part of water features in gardens; dormant during summer, but may remain evergreen in cultivation. Tubers contain orange-red or purplish pigments (arylphenalenones); also present in some other members of the family, but not found in any other organisms.

Hypoxis hemerocallidea (= *H. rooperi*)

Hypoxidaceae

E Hairy star-flower **A** Harigesterblom

Spring–Summer

Perennial herb, up to 400mm high, with a vertical rhizome; occurring in grassland. Leaves appearing before the flowers, arranged in three ranks, rather stiff and broad (10–50mm), arching outward, covered with long hairs. Flowers 5–23, on one or more erect or spreading stems; tepals six, bright yellow, hairy on the back.

Flowers open in the morning, close to midday. Rhizome with yellow flesh, used in traditional medicine. Once promoted by the popular press under the name 'African potato' as a 'miracle cure' for, among others, arthritis and prostate cancer. An anticancer compound has indeed been isolated from the plant. Also contains plant sterols, which have a proven beneficial effect on the immune system, but these are also present in fresh fruit and vegetables.

BRAAM VAN WYK & SASA MALAN

Hypoxis rigidula

Hypoxidaceae

E Silver-leaved star-flower **A** Silverblaarsterblom

Spring–Summer

Perennial herb, usually with a single, stiffly erect shoot, up to 1m high, with a fleshy vertical rhizome; occurring in grassland. Leaves basal, ± erect, 500–1,400 × 3–15mm, folded upward along midrib, overlapping to form a stem-like base, with short and often silver hairs. Flowers ± 40mm in diameter; tepals six, bright yellow, hairy on the back.

Being a vertical stem, the rhizome grows in length at the top; were it not for certain adaptations, it would soon emerge above ground. As in other members of the genus, the rhizome contains contractile roots. These roots can shorten considerably in length, thus pulling the rhizome down to maintain it at a particular level below the soil. In addition, the rhizome progressively dies at the bottom. Leaves formerly used to make a strong rope.

Bobartia orientalis

E Common bobartia **A** Gewone blombiesie

Iridaceae
Spring

Rush-like, tussock-forming perennial herb, up to 1.3m high, with a woody rhizome; occurring in fynbos, renosterveld and grassland. Leaves 2–8 per flowering stem, cylindrical, 1.2–2.5mm in diameter, ± as long as stems. Flowers crowded in dense, ± globose heads at the ends of erect, flowering stems, subtended by a usually green and erect spathe; perianth yellow with six segments, the outer ones 11–22 × 3.5–9mm, the inner ones slightly smaller, yellow.

Grows in profusion in recently burnt areas; flowering stimulated by fire. Leaves very tough and avoided by livestock; plants proliferate and may become dominant in severely overgrazed veld. Leaves used for making brooms. *B. indica* has flexible leaves that are much longer than the flowering stems and larger outer tepals.

Moraea fugax (= *M. edulis*)

E Edible moraea **A** Wituintjie

Iridaceae
Spring

Perennial herb, up to 400mm high, with a corm; occurring in karroid areas and fynbos, usually in sandy places. Leaves one or two, inserted high on the stem, immediately below the first branch, channelled, much longer than the stem, trailing. Flowers in a compact, branched inflorescence, iris-like, yellow, blue or white, strongly scented.

Flowers very short-lived, lasting about half the day. Corms are edible, pleasant-tasting, and are used in many traditional recipes. An important food source for the first human inhabitants of the Western Cape. Wash corms to remove soil, cook in salty water till soft, remove from tunics and eat; or, transfer to boiling milk, add a little corn or maize meal, flavour with orange or naartjie peel. Also eaten by various animals such as porcupines, mole rats and baboons.

JOHN MANNING

Moraea pallida (= *Homeria pallida*)
E Yellow tulp **A** Geeltulp

Iridaceae
Spring–Summer

A slender, erect perennial herb, up to 500mm high, with a corm; occurring in grassland and karroid vegetation, often on clayey soils in damp places. Leaf solitary, up to 1m long, 5–15mm wide, grooved. Flowers borne along an erect, unbranched or sparsely branched stem; tepals six, spreading ± on the same plane, usually yellow, with brownish speckles at base; style branches flattened, petal-like.

Leaves tough and fibrous, pleated when fresh to make whips and rope. Plants proliferate in overgrazed areas. Toxic to livestock in both fresh and dried state, the main toxic principles being bufadienolides. Death generally occurs 24–48 hours after ingestion of plants. Corms eaten with impunity by spring hares and pigs. *Moraea* comprises about 200 species, the ones with poisonous corms formerly classified as *Homeria*.

Moraea spathulata
E Large yellow moraea **A** Grootgeeltulp

Iridaceae
All year

Erect, usually clump-forming, perennial herb, up to 900mm high, with a corm; occurring in open grassland, often in rocky places. Leaf solitary, ± flat above, up to 1m × 15mm, straggling, usually dried at the tip. Flowers borne near the ends of tall, erect stems, iris-like; tepals yellow, with deep yellow nectar guides at the base of the outer tepals.

Plants in different geographical areas have very variable flowering times. An attractive and easily grown garden plant, even in areas with mild frost. Leaves fibrous; used to make rope. Poisonous to livestock. *M. alticola*, the largest and most robust species in the genus, is found above 2,200m in the Drakensberg. It has the basal parts surrounded by coarse, fibrous tunics, and the flowers are pale yellow.

Monopsis lutea
🇪 Yellow monopsis **🇦 Geel-monopsis**

Lobeliaceae
Summer

Perennial herb, with creeping or straggling stems, up to 300mm high; occurring in fynbos and coastal vegetation, invariably in damp places such as seepage areas or along streams. Leaves alternate, narrow; margin toothed. Flowers solitary, axillary or terminal, two-lipped with three petals bent upward and two downward, ± 20mm in diameter, bright yellow; corolla tube concealing the staminal tube and style, split to the base between the two lower lobes.

Generic name derived from the Greek *monos* = one and *opsis* = appearance, probably alluding to the corolla, which is almost regular in some species; specific name from the Latin *luteus* = deep yellow. Related to *Lobelia*, which usually has a blue or purple two-lipped corolla with the three-lobed lip facing downward.

Gossypium herbaceum
🇪 Wild cotton **🇦 Wildekatoen**

Malvaceae
Summer–Autumn

Straggly perennial shrub or scrambler, up to 2m high; occurring in hot, frost-free, low-elevation bushveld (common in mopane veld). Leaves stalked, alternate, ± rounded in outline, deeply 5–7-lobed, heart-shaped at the base. Flowers solitary in leaf axils; lower calyx whorl of three leaf-like segments, with deeply incised margins; upper calyx whorl short, cup-shaped; petals five, free, bright yellow, with a dark maroon centre, fading to orange. Fruit a capsule, 15–20mm in diameter, dehiscent; seeds covered with white cotton wool.

Plants are particularly conspicuous during the fruiting stage. Cotton from seed used by birds for lining their nests. Distant relative (even parent) of cultivated cotton (mainly cultivars of *G. hirsutum*), the most important natural fibre in the world today.

Hibiscus calophyllus
E Wild stockrose **A** Wildestokroos

Malvaceae
Summer

Shrubby perennial herb, up to 2m high; occurring in bushveld and riverine bush, often in shady or moist places. Leaves ± circular, rarely 3–5-lobed, up to 120mm in diameter, velvety; base heart-shaped; margin toothed; stalk up to 50mm long. Flowers solitary in leaf axils, up to 120mm in diameter, yellow with a dark maroon centre; lower calyx whorl of five segments, relatively broad in the middle, tapering to a long hair-like tip; upper calyx whorl with lobes ovate to ovate-lanceolate, usually three-veined, joined to nearly halfway.

About 55 species of *Hibiscus* occur in the region. In *H. lunarifolius* the lower calyx segments are usually broadest near the base, and the flowers lack a dark centre. *H. engleri* has 3–5-lobed leaves, hairs that create extreme irritation and a lower calyx of 7–10 segments.

Hibiscus cannabinus
E Kenaf **A** Kenaf

Malvaceae
Summer

Erect annual herb, up to 2m high; stems with scattered, often purplish prickles; occurring in bushveld, often as a weed in cultivated lands or other disturbed places. Leaves ± rounded in outline, 3–7-lobed, up to 150mm in diameter, with a few minute prickles on the veins; margin toothed; stalk up to 22mm long, with prominent, nectar-secreting gland on the undersurface near the base of the midrib (visited by ants). Flowers solitary, axillary, or in terminal racemes, up to 100mm in diameter, pale yellow or cream with a very dark purple centre.

Commercially grown for its strong jute-like bark fibre ('kenaf' or 'Deccan hemp'), especially in India and southeastern Europe. Leaves, flowers and young fruit cooked as a green vegetable. Seed oil used medicinally and in oil lamps.

Conicosia pugioniformis

🇪 Large pigsroot 🇦 Gansies

Mesembryanthemaceae

Spring

Sprawling perennial or biennial succulent, up to 400mm high, with a taproot; occurring in strandveld and karroid vegetation, usually in deep sand or disturbed places. Leaves opposite, elongated, ± three-sided. Flowers solitary, on stout stalks, ± 100mm in diameter, unpleasantly scented; petals thread-like, numerous, arranged in several whorls, yellow. Capsules large, cone-shaped, with 12 or more chambers.

Flowers open in the afternoon and close at sunset; often visited by beetles. The capsules are unusual among mesembs in that the valves open under dry conditions to release the seed. In most other groups the capsules are closed when dry and open when wet. Naturalised as a weed in parts of Australia. *C. elongata*, the only other species, has tuberous roots and cylindrical leaves.

Grielum humifusum

🇪 Common grielum 🇦 Pietsnot

Neuradaceae

Spring

Prostrate annual herb, with creeping stems radiating from a fleshy taproot; occurring on sandy soils in karroid vegetation and strandveld, often along roadsides and in disturbed areas. Leaves divided into broad segments, with fine woolly hairs below. Flowers produced in abundance, 20–30mm in diameter, shiny lemon yellow, with a white ring in the centre.

A showy component of the spectacular mass flowering spring displays in Namaqualand and elsewhere in the Western and Northern Cape. Flowers opening in bright sunshine. The fleshy roots are very slimy, hence the Afrikaans common name; it is a favourite food of the duiker and was formerly also extensively used as food by humans. *G. grandiflorum* has finely divided leaves with silvery hairs, and shiny, dark yellow flowers with a green centre.

Oenothera jamesii

E Giant evening primrose **A** Reuse aandblom

Onagraceae

Spring–Summer

Erect, branched, herbaceous perennial, up to 2m high; occurring in moist, disturbed places, often along roadsides. Leaves alternate, broadly lanceolate to elliptical, ± stalkless; margin shallowly toothed. Flowers solitary in leaf axils, up to 80mm in diameter, with a calyx tube 60–100mm long; petals four, bright yellow, fading to pinkish. Capsules ± cylindrical, ± 25 × 10mm, dehiscent, with numerous tiny seeds.

A native of North America. Evening-primrose oil, a rich source of gammalinolenic acid, is extracted from the seed of members of the genus. It is used against arthritis and many other ailments, notably premenstrual tension and atopic eczema. It is also extensively used in cosmetic skin products and as a dietary supplement. Seed of some species still viable after 80 years.

Disa woodii

E Wood's disa **A** Wood-se-disa

Orchidaceae

Winter–Spring

Stout, unbranched, erect perennial herb, up to 700mm high, with a tuber; occurring in grassland, usually in damp and marshy places, also on roadside embankments. Leaves sheathing at the base, extending up the stem, ± fleshy. Flowers small, crowded in an elongated, cylindrical, terminal spike, bright yellow; outer three petal-like sepals 5–7mm long, the dorsal one with a slender spur ± 1.5mm long.

Plants usually grow in large colonies and are visible from afar. Orchids have a complicated floral structure; the single stamen has become united with the style and stigma to form a structure called the column. Pollen grouped into masses (pollinia). Flowers of *D. chrysostachya* are more orange in colour, and the spur is inflated and much longer than the dorsal sepal. *D. polygonoides* has bright red flowers.

Eulophia angolensis (= *Lissochilus buchanani*)

Orchidaceae
Summer

E Tall marsh orchid **A** Reuse vlei-orgidee

Robust, erect perennial herb, up to 2m high, with a tuberous rhizome; occurring in grassland, invariably in marshy places. Leaves basal, stiffly erect, up to 900 × 50mm, longitudinally pleated. Flowers in terminal racemes, bright lemon-yellow, pleasantly scented; sepals petal-like, three, erect, sometimes tinged olive and purplish brown; lower petal (lip) with 3–5 narrow ridges and a short basal pouch (spur), partly covered by the two lateral petals.

Plants often grow in large colonies and are a spectacular sight with their tall inflorescences that stand well above the marsh vegetation. The inflorescence is produced next to the leaf-bearing shoot. Rhizome infusions are taken as love charm emetics by young Zulu men. About 42 species of *Eulophia* are native to the region.

Oxalis pes-caprae

Oxalidaceae
Autumn–Spring

E Yellow sorrel **A** Langbeensuring

Perennial herb, up to 400mm high, with or without a naked stem below the leaves, with a tuberous bulb; occurring in semidesert vegetation and fynbos, often among rocks or as a weed of cultivation. Leaves in a rosette, trifoliolate; leaflets wedge-shaped, deeply lobed at the tip; stalk up to 120mm long. Flowers in heads of 3–20 at the ends of tall, ± erect stalks, drooping in bud; corolla broadly funnel-shaped, with five petals, yellow; sepals often tipped with orange warts.

Leaves and flowers are cooked, mixed with goats' milk when cold, strained and served as a tasty beverage. Used in many other traditional recipes; bulbs also edible. An introduced weed in many parts of the world, especially troublesome in Australia. Grazed in large quantities, plants may cause oxalic-acid poisoning in sheep.

Argemone ochroleuca (= A. subfusiformis)

E White Mexican poppy **A** Bloudissel

Papaveraceae

Spring–Summer

Blue-green, spiny annual herb, up to 1m high, with a distinctive unpleasant odour when crushed; occurring throughout the region as a weed of disturbed places. Leaves stalkless, deeply pinnately lobed; margin toothed, teeth ending in hard yellowish spines. Flowers solitary, terminal, ± 50mm in diameter; petals pale cream to almost white; stamens many, yellow. Fruit a spiny capsule, dehiscent.

A native of Mexico, now a cosmopolitan weed. Often a pioneer on bare ground, thus preventing soil erosion. Spiny fruit and leaf lobes may contaminate wool. Plants contain a yellow milky latex and toxic alkaloids. *A. mexicana*, also a weed from tropical America, has thin-textured green leaves and bright yellow flowers. It has a more restricted distribution along the east coast.

Leucadendron salignum

E Common sunshine conebush **A** Knoppiesgeelbos

Proteaceae

Autumn–Spring

Many-stemmed shrub, usually ± 1m high, with a rootstock; occurring in fynbos, often in extensive stands. Leaves ± stalkless, 20–60 × 3–6mm; base slightly twisted. Flowers small, yellowish or reddish, clustered in roundish heads, male and female ones on different plants; heads surrounded by showy yellow, cream or red involucral leaves, these being slightly longer than the foliage leaves. Female heads develop into globose, cone-like fruiting heads that stay on the plant until after a fire; they then open to release small, winged fruit.

Female plants tend to be smaller than males and are less branched with larger leaves; a difference perhaps due to the fact that females devote more resources to seed production. The more than 80 species of *Leucadendron* are all confined to South Africa, most occurring in the Cape Floristic Kingdom.

COLIN PATERSON-JONES

Leucospermum cuneiforme

E Wart-stemmed pincushion **A** Gewone speldekussing

Proteaceae

All year

Many-stemmed shrub, up to 2m high, arising from an underground rootstock; occurring in fynbos. Basal parts of old stems with warts and pustules. Leaves are stalkless, oblanceolate; tip rounded, with 3–10 glandular teeth. Flower heads are yellow, and made up of numerous flowers with long, colourful styles; the bracts are inconspicuous.

While the flowers are still in bud, the anthers deposit their pollen on a sticky swelling (pollen presenter) near the tip of the style. When the buds open, the perianth and stamens curl back to expose the long styles. This mechanism of pollen presentation ensures adequate transfer of pollen to pollinators, in this species mainly birds. The ± 50 species of pincushion are largely confined to South Africa; many are grown as cut flowers and garden ornamentals.

COLIN PATERSON-JONES

Ranunculus baurii

E Large-leaved buttercup **A** Grootblaarrenonkel

Ranunculaceae

Summer

Perennial herb, up to 1.2m high, with a rootstock; occurring in grassland and along forest margins, usually in wet places. Leaves roundish, 50–200mm in diameter; veins whitish on upper surface; margin closely and bluntly toothed, red; stalk attached to centre of blade, 100–450mm long, hollow. Flowers solitary in small plants, many in branched inflorescences in large plants; petals 13–15, shiny yellow; stamens numerous.

Characteristic species of the high Drakensberg; leaf size diminishes with elevation. The genus is known for its toxic compounds, although nothing appears to be published on the chemistry of this species. Generic name comes from the Latin *rana* = frog, as many members grow in wet places where frogs abound. Seven species occur in the region.

LAL GREEN

LAL GREEN

Gnidia capitata
E Curry flower **A** Kerrieblom

Thymelaeaceae

Spring

Herbaceous perennial shrublet, up to 500mm high, with a tuberous rootstock; occurring in grassland. Stems reddish brown. Leaves stalkless, narrowly elliptic, ± 30 × 6mm, sharply pointed, often bluish green, ± hairless. Flowers in lax, few-flowered heads, without a prominently elongated subtending stalk; sepals five, petal-like, mustard yellow; petals small, scale-like.

Flowering stimulated by veld fires; a typical pre-rain flower of the Grassland Biome. Used as a snuff to treat headaches; also utilised for magical purposes. Often associated with, and flowering at the same time as, *G. caffra*, a species characterised by sparsely hairy leaves and lemon-yellow flowers. Common names allude to the floral colour. About 100 species of *Gnidia* occur in the region; all have very tough bark.

Gnidia kraussiana
E Lesser yellow head **A** Harige gifbossie

Thymelaeaceae

Spring

Perennial shrublet, up to 500mm high, with annual shoots from a fleshy tuber; occurring in grassland. Stems robust, hairy. Leaves elliptic, ± 30 × 10mm, sharply pointed, sparsely to densely hairy; margin often fringed with hairs; stalk up to 2mm long. Flowers in compact heads of 18–35 flowers, the latter carried on a prominently elongated, leafless stalk; sepals petal-like, yellow; petals scale-like.

Flowering stimulated by veld fires in late winter. Plants are highly toxic and have been used as a fish and arrow poison; contain poisonous substances known to cause skin tumours. Decoctions of the tuber are nevertheless widely employed to treat a variety of ailments. Also used as a medicine to heal fractured limbs in livestock; injected by means of a hollow reed into the limb near the fracture.

Lippia scaberrima
E Makwassie bush **A** Makwassiebossie

Verbenaceae
Summer

Rounded shrublet, up to 600mm high, with annual shoots from a woody rootstock; occurring in grassland and bushveld. Leaves opposite, ± elliptic, coarsely hairy; margin toothed. Flowers very small, cream, densely clustered in rounded or usually elongated axillary racemes; bracts prominent, green. Crushed plants are strongly and pleasantly ± mint-scented.

An infusion of the leaves is widely used as a herbal tea to treat various ailments, with proven efficiency when used as a mouthwash against gum infections. North West town of Makwassie claimed (incorrectly so!) to have been named after original San name for this species, hence the common names. Four species of *Lippia* occur in the region, all highly aromatic. *L. rehmannii* is a small, lemon-scented shrublet. *L. javanica*, an erect, ± woody shrub up to 2m high, is common in high-rainfall bushveld and grassland areas.

Sisyndite spartea
E Desert broom **A** Woestynbesem

Zygophyllaceae
Spring–Summer

Many-branched shrub, up to 2.5m high, with grey-green twigs; occurring in semidesert areas, often on rocky outcrops or along dry watercourses. Leaves compound, ± opposite, 70–300mm long; leaflets obovate, tiny (20 × 8mm). Flowers usually solitary in forks of branches, cup-shaped; petals five, broadly obovate, yellow, with orange-yellow lines. Seed capsules with long, fluffy cream hairs.

What appear to be leaves are in fact leaflets (they lack axillary buds); terminal branchlets are the main axes of pinnate leaves. The only member of the genus; restricted to the Northern Cape and southern Namibia. Flowers close at night, often providing a shelter for the males of one of its pollinators, the long-tongued solitary bee (*Parafidelia pallidula*), which does not have burrows of its own.

ROBERT ARCHER

ZIETS ZIETSMAN

Tribulus terrestris
E Devil's thorn **A** Dubbeltjie

Zygophyllaceae
Summer

Annual herb with much-branched, creeping shoots; widespread, often a weed in disturbed areas. Leaves opposite, usually with one of a pair shorter than the other, pinnately compound, without a terminal leaflet. Flowers solitary in leaf axils, 6–10mm in diameter; petals five; stamens 10; pistil with style absent. Fruit woody, with sharp spines.

A common indigenous weed. Flowers open after sunrise and close by midday. Despite being highly nutritious to livestock, the plant is at times the cause of a major hepatogenous photosensitivity disease in sheep, known as *geeldikkop*, 'yellow thick head'. Outbreaks of the disease usually occur sporadically when wilted plants are grazed during hot, dry spells following summer rains, especially in the Karoo. Ostrich eat the spiny fruit with impunity.

Zygophyllum morgsana (= *Roepera morgsana*)
E Tortoise bush **A** Skilpadbos

Zygophyllaceae
Winter–Spring

Robust perennial shrub, up to 1.5m high; occurring in karroid vegetation and fynbos, especially common in strandveld. Branches covered with lichens in areas with high incidence of fog. Leaves bifoliolate, ± succulent; leaflets obovate; stalk 12–25mm long. Flowers in pairs at the ends of branches; petals four, free, pale yellow, with a dark purplish blotch at the base. Fruit pendulous, with four prominent, membranous wings.

Crushed leaves are unpleasantly scented; apparently toxic and the cause of diarrhoea in livestock. Powdered seeds are used as an old Cape remedy for convulsions, paralyses and 'strokes'. More than 50 species of *Zygophyllum* (sometimes treated as *Roepera*) occur in South Africa. The group is easily recognised by the bifoliolate leaves. Some species are important grazing plants in the arid parts of the region.

Thunbergia alata

E Black-eyed Susan **A** Swartoognooi

Acanthaceae
Summer

Herbaceous creeper, with slender, twining stems that sprout from a perennial root system; occurring along forest margins and in bushy places. Leaves hairy; base heart-shaped; petioles winged. Flowers on slender stalks and subtended by two small, leaf-like bracts, trumpet-shaped, bright orange, with inner surface of the tube dark purplish black.

Attractive garden plant; quick growing and self-seeding, often treated as an annual. Genus name commemorates the Swedish botanist, Carl Peter Thunberg (1743–1828), one of Linnaeus' pupils and often described as the 'father of Cape botany'. His famous book, *Flora Capensis* (1823), contains the results of three years (1772–1775) of travelling and botanical collecting in the region, including the description of many plant species new to science.

Clivia caulescens

E Escarp bush lily **A** Platorandboslelie

Amaryllidaceae
Spring–Summer

Evergreen perennial herb, up to 1m high, with creeping rhizomes; occurring in moist, humus-rich places in the shade of forest or large boulders, sometimes growing on trees or rocks. Leaves strap-shaped, 300–400 × 30mm, dark green. Flowers in umbels on erect stalks, tubular, drooping, deep orange to red, with a yellowish-green tip. Fruit a berry, red.

A shade-loving species, widely cultivated in gardens. It is characterised by a length of thick stem above ground, which bears the leaves. Extensive stands may be seen in the 'rainforest' at the God's Window lookout along the Drakensberg Escarpment near Graskop in Mpumalanga. Very similar to *C. gardenii* and *C. nobilis*, by which it is replaced further south in the forests of KwaZulu-Natal and the Eastern Cape.

Clivia miniata
E Bush lily **A** Boslelie

Amaryllidaceae

Spring

 Evergreen perennial herb, up to 1m high, with creeping rhizomes; occurring in moist places in the shade of forest, often growing on rocks. Leaves strap-shaped, 300–400 × 30mm. Flowers in umbels on erect stalks, bell-shaped, spreading, orange with a whitish-yellow centre.

All six species of *Clivia* are confined to southern Africa. This species has the most spectacular flowers. An extremely popular garden or pot plant for shady situations; extensively cultivated worldwide. A cool winter stimulates flowering. Cultivars include forms with bright yellow, whitish, dark orange-red and bicoloured flowers. Although rhizomes of all bush lilies contain alkaloids and are extremely toxic, plants of this species, as well as *C. nobilis*, are widely used in traditional medicine.

Aloe ferox
E Bitter aloe **A** Bitteraalwyn

Asphodelaceae

Winter

 Single-stemmed, unbranched leaf succulent; stem densely covered with old dry leaves; occurring in valley bushveld (thicket), karroid vegetation, coastal bush and grassland, usually on rocky hillsides. Leaves with or without spines on both surfaces; margin with brownish-red teeth. Inflorescence branched; flower spikes erect; flowers golden orange to scarlet, rarely white, with tips of inner perianth lobes usually brown or black.

Yellowish sap from the leaves is the source of 'Cape aloes', an intensely bitter drug widely used in pharmaceutical preparations, especially for its purgative properties. The jelly-like leaf pulp is used in cosmetic preparations and to prepare a pleasant-tasting health drink. *A. candelabrum*, found in KwaZulu-Natal, tends to have white-tipped perianth lobes.

Aloe marlothii
E Mountain aloe **A** Bergaalwyn

Asphodelaceae
Winter

Single-stemmed, unbranched leaf succulent; stem densely covered with old dry leaves; occurring in bushveld, usually on rocky hillsides. Leaves usually with many spines on both surfaces; margin with reddish-brown teeth. Inflorescence branched; flower spikes carried ± horizontally, with the flowers pointing in the same direction (upward); flowers purplish in bud, opening yellow, orange or bright red, with purple stamens; inner tepals tipped dull purple.

Ash from the dried leaves is mixed with tobacco snuff. The leaves and sap are used medicinally. *A. spectabilis*, from central KwaZulu-Natal, has spikes that are erect or suberect with the flowers evenly distributed around the axis, and with the tips of the inner tepals being a glossy black.

Kniphofia linearifolia
E Common marsh poker **A** Gewone moerasvuurpyl

Asphodelaceae
Summer–Autumn

Robust rhizomatous perennial, up to 1.8m high; occurring in grassland, usually as dense stands in marshy places. Leaves long and narrow, at first erect, usually bending back under their weight toward maturity, strongly keeled, yellow-green to dull green. Flowers borne well above the reflexed leaves, in dense, ± elongated terminal spikes, drooping, orange-red, pinkish red or dull red in bud, greenish yellow to yellow when open; bracts oblong to blunt or rounded.

Most widespread red-hot poker in the region. Very similar to *K. praecox*, a species extensively grown in gardens, which is characterised by sharply pointed, lanceolate bracts. Closely related to *K. rooperi* and *K. uvaria*, both of which have roundish flowering spikes. Flowers visited by sunbirds, bees and butterflies.

Arctotis fastuosa (= *Venidium fastuosum*)

E Bitter marigold **A** Bittergousblom

Asteraceae

Winter–Spring

Annual herb, up to 600mm high; occurring in semidesert areas, often in profusion on sandy soils. Leaves deeply lobed, up to 150mm long, sparsely covered with woolly, white hairs. Flower heads (see page 142) up to 60mm in diameter, borne singly on an erect, leafy stalk; ray florets arranged in two series, orange in colour, those of the inner series with a conspicuous dark brown to black blotch at the base; disc floret black in bud, yellow when open; involucral bracts covered in a white wool.

As one of about 66 species of *Arctotis* in southern Africa, this species, with its large, brilliant flowers, creates spectacular spring shows in Namaqualand; it is often grown in gardens. Common names refer to the bitter taste imparted to the milk of cattle that have grazed on the plants.

Dimorphotheca sinuata

E Namaqualand daisy **A** Namakwalandse madeliefie

Asteraceae

Winter–Spring

Sprawling annual herb; occurring in semidesert areas, particularly on disturbed and sandy sites. Leaves simple, hairless; margin shallowly toothed. Flower heads (see page 142) solitary, up to 80mm in diameter; ray florets in a single series, orange-yellow.

Prominent constituents of the brilliant orange mass displays of spring flowers in Namaqualand. Flowers only open fully in bright sunshine. Seeds of disc florets flat and thin-walled with papery wings. They are rather fragile and germinate readily the next rainy season. Seeds of ray florets elongated with thick, hard walls. These thick-walled seeds may remain dormant for several years, thus providing protection against drought, which seedlings of the mass-germinating thin-walled seeds seldom survive. Cultivated in gardens and parks worldwide.

Gorteria diffusa
E Beetle daisy **A** Kewermadeliefie

Asteraceae
Winter–Spring

Sprawling annual herb, up to 300mm high; occurring in semidesert areas, often in dense stands. Leaves usually unlobed, roughly hairy above, white-felted below. Flower heads (see page 142) borne singly on erect stalks, 20–35mm in diameter; ray florets deep orange above, purplish below, two or more with a conspicuous black and dark brown blotch, usually marked with green and white dots toward the base; disc florets yellow; involucral bracts long and spiny.

The peculiar dark markings on the ray florets mimic certain beetles. The markings are believed to serve a role in attracting specific beetle pollinators, and/or to repel destructive beetles. Another suggestion is that these black spots serve to attract a bee fly pollinator, *Megapalpus nitidus*, through visual sexual mimicry.

Ursinia calenduliflora
E Mountain marigold **A** Bergmagriet

Asteraceae
Winter–Spring

Annual herb, up to 360mm high; occurring in semidesert areas, often in dense stands on sandy soils and fallow fields. Leaves up to 50mm long, finely divided into narrow segments. Solitary flower heads (see page 142) borne on slender, erect stalks, drooping when young, 20–50mm in diameter; ray florets orange, usually with a purple base; disc florets yellow; involucral bracts in many rows, with conspicuous transparent tips. Fruit tipped by petal-like white scales.

One of the many species of orange and yellow daisies that, following good winter rains, covers the fields and mountains of the usually drab semidesert Namaqualand with a blanket of colour. There are about 35 species of *Ursinia* in the region; at least 14 occur in Namaqualand, with *U. cakilefolia* often abundant on fallow land.

GRETEL VAN ROOYEN

Begonia sutherlandii
E Wild orange begonia **A** Oranje-wildebegonia

Begoniaceae
Spring–Summer

Soft perennial herb, up to 1m high, with one or several somewhat fleshy stems from a small tuber; occurring mainly in shady and rocky places in forest, often forming large colonies, sometimes epiphytic on trees. Stems green, tinged red. Leaves thin-textured, up to 250 × 150mm, with a satiny sheen above; base asymmetrical; margin sharply toothed, frequently lobed as well. Flowers in axillary or terminal, many-flowered inflorescences, pale to deep orange. Fruit three-winged.

One of the most widespread of the African begonias, ranging from central through East Africa as far south as the Eastern Cape. As in other begonias, male and female flowers are borne separately, but on the same plant. Leaf and stem infusions are used to treat heartburn and other ailments.

Tecomaria capensis (= *Tecoma capensis*)
E Cape-honeysuckle **A** Kaapse kanferfoelie

Bignoniaceae
All year

Many-stemmed climbing shrub or, rarely, a small tree to 4m high; occurring in bushveld, thicket and along forest margins. Leaves opposite, pinnately compound. Leaflets with small hair tufts in axils of principal side veins below; margin scalloped or toothed. Flowers in terminal racemes, orange-red. Capsules pod-like, up to 130mm long, splitting to release many papery-winged seeds.

Sunbirds feast on the abundant nectar in the flower and also act as pollinators. The stigma is touch-sensitive, with the two lobes folding together when touched. Bark used medicinally. Widely cultivated as a garden ornamental, with many cultivars, including forms with yellow, red, pink and pale orange flowers. Related to the South and Central American genus *Tecoma*, some members of which are hummingbird-pollinated.

Crocosmia mathewsiana

E Mathews' crocosmia **A** Mathews-se-valentynsblom

Iridaceae
Summer

Erect, deciduous perennial, up to 1.8m high, with a corm; occurring in grassland, usually along the banks of mountain streams, in full sun or semishade. Leaves arranged in a fan, sword-shaped, usually more than 30mm wide. Flowers in a large, erect, laxly branched panicle, all pointing to one side; perianth bright reddish orange, tepals spreading; stamens with only anthers exserted from perianth tube.

A stunning plant. Threatened by commercial afforestation. Resembles *C. masonorum* from the Eastern Cape, which has tall, unbranched or sparingly branched flowering spikes, *C. aurea*, a smaller (up to 1m), shade-loving plant, has drooping golden orange flowers in unbranched or weakly branched spikes; cultivated in gardens worldwide, with a number of cultivars (garden montbrettias).

Gladiolus alatus

E Kalkoentjie **A** Kalkoentjie

Iridaceae
Spring

Erect perennial, up to 200mm high, with a corm; occurring singly or as small groups in fynbos and renosterveld of the winter-rainfall area, favouring stony sandstone or granitic soils. Leaves sword-shaped, strongly ribbed. Flowers in racemes, all turned in the same direction, orange, with the three lower petals yellow to greenish and tipped with orange, sweetly scented; upper petal more or less erect.

Apparently pollinated by the bee *Anthophora diversipes*. The common name *kalkoentjie* (= little turkey) alludes to the flowers, which resemble the wattles of a turkey (a *kalkoen* in Afrikaans). *G. speciosus* is very similar, but the upper petal is hooded. Also resembles *G. equitans* from Namaqualand, a species that has rather broad (15–45mm), not prominently ridged, spine-tipped leaves.

Gladiolus dalenii

Iridaceae

🇪 Wild gladiolus 🇦 Wildeswaardlelie

Spring–Summer

Erect perennial, up to 1.5m high, sprouting annually from a corm; occurring in grassland and bushveld, often in groups among rocks or in bush clumps. Leaves arranged in a fan, erect, 10–30mm wide, hairless, with prominent ribs. Flowers in erect spikes, large (60–80mm long), orange to red, with a yellow mark on each of the three lower petals.

The most widespread and common member of the more than 250 species of *Gladiolus*. Introduced during the late 1820s from KwaZulu-Natal to European gardens by the Dutch botanist, Cornelius Dalen. One of the parent species used in the breeding of the large-flowered *Gladiolus* cultivars that is of considerable importance in the cut-flower trade today. Widely used medicinally, although the corms contain toxic compounds, notably saponins.

Watsonia pillansii

Iridaceae

🇪 Large orange watsonia 🇦 Grootoranjepypie

Summer

Perennial plant, up to 1.2m high, with a corm; occurring in grassland and fynbos, often in rocky places. Leaves 4–6, strap-shaped, 12–18mm wide. Flowers usually 25–35 in an erect spike, arranged in two rows and pointing in opposite directions, bright orange to orange-red; perianth with three whitish ridges between the lower parts of the filaments.

Watsonia is a horticulturally important genus of more than 50 species, all confined to southern Africa. There are also species with attractive pink, red, purple, mauve or white flowers. When planting watsonias it is important to note whether the species are from the winter- or summer-rainfall area. Similar to *W. schlechteri*, a montane species with narrower (6–15mm) leaves from the southwestern and southern Western Cape.

Leonotis leonurus

E Wild dagga   **A** Wildedagga

Lamiaceae
Summer–Autumn

Robust perennial shrub, up to 2m high, with erect stems from a thick, woody base; occurring along forest margins and in grassland, often in rocky places and on stream banks. Leaves opposite; margin toothed. Flowers in successive, compact whorls, tubular, two-lipped, densely covered with orange hairs.

Parts of the plant, in particular the old seed-containing inflorescences, were once smoked for their narcotic properties. The common names are misleading as it is not at all related to the dagga or marijuana (*Cannabis sativa*) plant. Widely used in traditional medicine to treat a variety of ailments. The generic name, which means 'lion's ears' (from the Greek *leon* = lion + *otis* = ear), refers to the hairy upper lip of the flowers. Flowers pollinated mainly by sunbirds. Popular as a garden ornamental.

Leonotis nepetifolia

E Annual wild dagga   **A** Eenjarige wildedagga

Lamiaceae
Summer–Autumn

Slender, erect annual or short-lived perennial, up to 3m tall, slightly branched at the upper nodes only; occurring in bushveld, usually in disturbed sites such as fallow fields and along roadsides. Leaves opposite, broadly ovate with a distinct stalk, 50–200 × 40–150mm. Flowers in dense, spherical clusters grouped at intervals up the stem, tubular, two-lipped, densely covered with rather dull, pale orange hairs; calyx ± two-lipped, lobes spine-tipped.

A weedy indigenous species, widely distributed northwards in Africa as well as in other tropical parts of the world. Extensively used all over its range in traditional medicine for many different ailments. About eight species of *Leonotis* occur in South Africa, the flowers of which contain abundant nectar and are pollinated by sunbirds.

Salvia africana-lutea (= *S. aurea*)

E Golden sage **A Bruinsalie**

Lamiaceae
Winter–Spring

A much-branched, greyish perennial shrub, up to 2m high; occurring in fynbos and scrub, often on coastal dunes. Stems densely leafy, with minute orange-red dots. Leaves stalked, thick-textured, densely covered with grey hairs. Flowers in clusters, each comprising several two-flowered whorls; corolla golden brown, reddish brown or rarely purplish brown, upper lip ± 12mm long; calyx persistent after flowering, saucer-like, purplish-tinged; bracts broadly ovate or obovate, persistent.

The aromatic leaves are used in cooking to flavour food, especially fish, and in traditional medicine to treat colds and coughs. Sometimes confused with brown-flowered forms of *S. lanceolata*, a species with branched inflorescences, deciduous bracts and flowers with the upper lip ± 17mm long.

Papaver aculeatum

E Wild poppy **A Wildepapawer**

Papaveraceae
Summer

Prickly annual herb, up to 1.5m high, most parts covered with long, stiff, yellowish hairs and spines, and containing milky latex. Occurring in grassland and karroid shrubland, often in disturbed places. Leaves arranged in a basal rosette, or spaced along a sturdy, erect flowering stem; margin shallowly to deeply pinnately lobed. Flowers borne on long stalks, drooping in bud; petals crinkly, orange to salmon pink.

A biogeographical enigma in being the only member of *Papaver* indigenous to the southern hemisphere. It is also peculiar in that plants may suddenly appear at a spot in a particular season, only to vanish without a trace in subsequent years. A very variable species in growth form and floral colour; more than one taxon may be involved. Naturalised in Australia.

Strelitzia reginae
E Crane flower   **A** Kraanvoëlblom

Strelitziaceae
All year

A robust, stemless perennial, up to 1.5m high; occurring in coastal grassland, often in rocky places. Leaves distinctly stalked; blade up to 500 × 100mm. Flowers ± six in a spathe, opening one at a time; the outer three tepals are bright orange and serve for display, the inner three are blue, two being large, forming an arrow-like structure concealing the stamens and style, while the third one is much smaller concealing the nectary.

Flower pollination by perching weaver birds and, to a lesser extent, sunbirds. The blue arrow-like structure has two lobes at the base on which birds occasionally stand to feed on the nectar or orange tepals. The weight of the bird pushes the lobes apart, exposing the anthers, which dust the feet and underside of the bird with sticky pollen. A popular garden plant and cut flower worldwide.

Tricliceras longipedunculatum
E Roadside pimpernel   **A** Rooihaarbossie

Turneraceae
Spring–Summer

A herb up to 450mm high, sprouting annually from a perennial taproot; occurring in bushveld, often along roadsides or in fallow lands. Stems with long, reddish-purple hairs. Leaves stalkless, linear to oblong, with a few scattered, long, reddish hairs on the midrib below; margin smooth. Flowers in racemes of 7–15 flowers; petals bright orange above, yellowish below.

Each flower lasts only one day, but flowering extends over a long period. A rich source of toxic chemicals known as pentacyclic cyanogenic glycosides, the plants serve as food for the larvae of several butterflies of the genus *Acraea*. These compounds are accumulated by the butterfly larvae and eventually end up in the mature butterflies, thus rendering both stages toxic or distasteful to predators such as birds.

Anisotes rogersii

E Limpopo anisotes **A** Limpopo-anisotes

Acanthaceae
Summer–Autumn

Deciduous perennial shrublet, up to 1.5m high; occurring in hot, arid, frost-free areas, often in mopane or acacia woodland. Young branches round or angled, but not grooved, greyish. Leaves opposite or clustered on reduced shoots, narrowly elliptic or ovate, 30–80 × 15–35mm; stalk up to 2mm long. Flowers axillary, produced in clusters; corolla tubular, two-lipped, 38–60mm long, red to orange; upper lip slightly arched, with tip two-fid. Capsules obovoid, flattened, 25–30mm long, 8mm wide.

The species is locally abundant in the Limpopo River Valley. Following good rains, mass flowering of plants can turn the veld into a blaze of colour. Pollinated by sunbirds. *A. formosissimus*, from further north in southern Africa, has the new branches four-angled, grooved and greenish, with flowers in spikes.

PIET VAN WYK – AGFA

Crossandra greenstockii

E Bushveld crossandra **A** Bosveld-crossandra

Acanthaceae
Spring–Summer

Erect perennial herb, up to 300mm high, sprouting annually from a woody rootstock; occurring in bushveld. Leaves ± oval, mostly in a basal rosette, hairy, narrowing to a stalk-like base. Flowers in dense spikes, with the inflorescence stalk usually unbranched; corolla with a long, very narrow tube and a flaring, five-lobed lip, ± 20mm wide, bright orange-red; bracts large (25 × 18mm), overlapping, green, with long-stalked glandular hairs, margin with a few short teeth or smooth.

When the dry capsules are wetted by rain, they split explosively, ejecting the seed some distance from the plant. Upon wetting, flat hairs on the seed uncurl and become sticky, causing them to adhere to wet soil. Similar to *C. zuluensis*, which has almost hairless bracts and larger flowers (± 30mm wide).

Ammocharis coranica
E Sore-eye flower **A** Seeroogblom

Amaryllidaceae

Spring

 Deciduous perennial with a large bulb; occurring in grassland, bushveld and karroid vegetation, usually in groups. Leaves radiating on or near the ground, strap-shaped, older ones blunt-tipped (died back). Flowers in a globose head borne on a flattened stalk, sweetly scented; perianth silvery pink, segments recurved; anthers white.

Plants grow very old; larger ones may be well over 100 years. Bulb contains several poisonous alkaloids. Used for medicinal and magical purposes; fresh bulb scales are lightly fried and applied as a dressing to open wounds and boils. A paste prepared from the cooked bulb is used to repair cracks in clay pots. Caterpillars of the lily leaf miner (*Brithys crini pancratii*) often bore inside the leaf tissue, but they do not usually attack the bulb.

Boophane disticha
E Poison bulb **A** Kopseerblom

Amaryllidaceae

Spring

 Deciduous perennial; bulb partly exposed above the ground; occurring mainly in grassland and bushveld. Leaves erect, arranged in a conspicuous fan, greyish green, usually produced after flowering. Flowers in a globose head, deep pink, sweetly scented; flower stalks lengthen considerably during the fruiting stage to form a large ball.

Larger bulbs may be several centuries old. Dry fruiting heads roll about in the wind, dispersing the seeds in the manner of a tumble weed. Exposure to flowers may result in headaches and sore eyes (apparently caused by the penetrating scent). Bulb poisonous due to the presence of numerous alkaloids, although widely used in traditional medicine; bulb scales are a popular dressing for wounds, sometimes after being soaked in olive or linseed oil.

Brunsvigia radulosa

E Pink candelabra flower **A** Pienkkandelaarblom

Amaryllidaceae

Summer

Deciduous perennial with a large bulb; occurring in grassland, karroid vegetation and bushveld. Leaves ± four, pressed close to the ground, appearing with or after flowering. Flowers in an umbel at the end of a sturdy, erect stalk, bright pink; flower stalks lengthen considerably during fruiting.

Fruiting heads roll about in the wind, scattering the seed as they rotate. Bulb used medicinally. Genus with ± 20 species, mainly southern African. Flowers pinkish red or crimson in *B. grandiflora* and *B. natalensis*. Leaves 10–15 and erect in the former, 2–5 and semi-erect in the latter. Both occur in the eastern and northeastern parts of the region and are summer-growing. *B. orientalis*, a red-flowered winter-growing species from the Western Cape, usually has the flower stalks tinged with red.

Crinum bulbispermum

E Vaal River lily **A** Hoëveldse vleilelie

Amaryllidaceae

Spring

Perennial, with a large bulb; occurring in grassland, usually along rivers and in marshy places. Leaves arching, strap-shaped, folded upward along the midrib; margin often wavy. Flowers clustered at the end of a tall, sturdy, erect inflorescence stalk, ± drooping when open; perianth white or pale to dark pink, with a dark pink keel; anthers greyish or pale brown. Fruits large with many roundish, fleshy green seeds, tipped by a scar.

Attractive garden plant. The fleshy seeds germinate readily without water, even while still in the fruit. Bulb highly poisonous due to the presence of various alkaloids; extensively used in traditional medicine, usually in small amounts and mixed with other ingredients. Similar to *C. macowanii*, which tends to have black anthers.

BRAAM VAN WYK & SASA MALAN

Crinum delagoense
E **Candy-striped crinum** A **Gestreepte vleilelie**

Amaryllidaceae

Spring

Perennial with a large bulb; occurring in coastal grassland and in low-elevation bushveld, usually on sandy soils. Leaves sprawling on the ground, strap-shaped, ± flat; margin with fine hairs. Flowers clustered at the end of a short, sturdy, arching inflorescence stalk, ± drooping when open; perianth white to pink, with a dark pink keel; anthers greyish or pale brown. Fruits large, pinkish red, tipped by a scar, with many roundish, fleshy seeds.

Conspicuous in coastal grassland of Maputaland. Attractive garden plant; flowers having a distinct striped appearance. Bulb used in traditional remedies to treat people and cattle. Similar in habit to *C. graminicola*, a species of Highveld grassland, which has ± uniformly deep pink flowers and fruit tipped by an elongated protuberance (beak).

Scadoxus puniceus
E **Red paintbrush** A **Rooikwas**

Amaryllidaceae

Spring

Deciduous perennial with a bulbous rhizome; occurring in grassland, bushveld and along forest margins, usually in rocky or shady places. Leaves erect, clasping at the base to form a short false stem; margin wavy; midrib distinct; leaf stalk purple-spotted. Flowers in a dense cluster ('brush') surrounded by large bracts; perianth indistinct; filaments conspicuous, scarlet; anthers yellow. Fruit a berry, red.

Bulbs poisonous, used in traditional medicine. *S. membranaceous*, from forest along the east coast, also has a congested inflorescence enclosed by large bracts, but it lacks a false stem. *S. multiflorus* has flowers with longer stalks and well-developed spreading tepals, resulting in more rounded inflorescences; an attractive container plant for shady places.

Pachypodium succulentum
E Mountain kambroo **A** Bergkambroo

Apocynaceae

Spring

Spiny, succulent, perennial shrublet, up to 600mm high, with milky latex and a large, half-submerged tuber; occurring in arid karroid vegetation. Leaves stalkless, alternate or in tufts, linear to linear-lanceolate, green and hairy above, with a white wool below; stipules spiny, borne on a cushion around base of leaf. Flowers in terminal clusters, crimson or shades of pink, rarely white, usually with a darker stripe; corolla lobes tapering to a point, 8–18mm long. Fruit elongated, paired, appearing horn-like.

The turnip-shaped tuber is edible. It is either consumed fresh, or used to brew an alcoholic beer or to prepare a yeast for baking bread. A pleasantly flavoured jam is cooked from young tubers. *P. bispinosum* from the Eastern Cape has shorter (5–7mm long) and more rounded corolla lobes.

Hoodia gordonii
E Baboon ghaap **A** Bobbejaanghaap

Asclepiadaceae

Summer

Erect, leafless, succulent perennial up to 750mm high, with a watery latex; occurring in semidesert vegetation, often in extensive colonies. Stems thick, cylindrical, with 11–17 longitudinal ridges bearing regularly spaced tubercles tipped by greyish or brownish spines. Flowers ± circular, flat and saucer-shaped, produced in profusion near tips of stems, large (50–100mm in diameter), flesh-coloured to purple-red with darker veins, unpleasantly scented.

The flowers are pollinated by flies. Stems used in traditional medicine. The specific name honours the pioneering Dutch explorer and naturalist Colonel R.J. Gordon (1743–1795), who first collected the plant, supposedly in the vicinity of Upington between 1778 and 1780. He also painted the species; the original painting is now in the Rijksmuseum, Amsterdam.

Microloma sagittatum
🇪 Pink kannetjies 🇦 Pienkkannetjies

Asclepiadaceae
Winter–Spring

Twining perennial herb with slender stems and milky latex; occurring in semidesert vegetation, usually in rocky places. Leaves opposite, narrow, arrow-shaped, up to 25mm long; margin recurved. Flowers in loose clusters, ± 7mm long, erect; corolla tubular, five-angled, pink, the petals hardly spreading (flowers appear closed).

Pollinated by sunbirds, which carry the sticky pollinia (see page 141) on the tongue from one flower to another. The flowers contain abundant sweet nectar. This is sucked from the flowers by children, hence the common names (in Afrikaans *kannetjies* = little cans). Plants are very palatable to sheep and goats. *M. namaquense* has red flowers with the tips of the petals rounded and overlapping in a spiral rosette. *M. calycinum* has large, spreading, petal-like, reddish-pink sepals.

Aloe arborescens
🇪 Krantz aloe 🇦 Kransaalwyn

Asphodelaceae
Autumn–Winter

Much-branched succulent shrub or small tree, up to 3m high; occurring in high-rainfall grassland and forest areas, usually in rocky places. Leaves in terminal, somewhat obliquely disposed rosettes, dull greyish or bluish green; spineless on both surfaces; margin with pale teeth. Flowers usually in unbranched, erect spikes, 200–300mm long, 2–4 per rosette; scarlet, orange, pink or yellow.

A decorative garden plant, easily propagated from cuttings or truncheons; probably the most widely cultivated aloe in the world. It is also grown as a live fence around cattle kraals. Pulp from leaves is used medicinally, with proven success against X-ray burns. Closely related to *A. mutabilis* (Gauteng to Polokwane), a smaller plant with bicoloured racemes (buds red, open flowers yellow).

Aloe claviflora

Asphodelaceae
Spring

E Kraal aloe **A** Kraalaalwyn

Perennial succulent, with leaves in a ± asymmetrical rosette; stems absent or very short; occurring in karroid vegetation, in dense groups or circular patches on hill slopes or in flat, stony areas. Leaves greyish green, rough-textured, with a few spines on the lower surface toward the tip; margin with brown spines. Inflorescences produced at an angle, often almost horizontal to the ground; flowers club-shaped, arranged in densely flowered, bicoloured racemes, buds and young flowers bright red, older ones yellow fading to white; perianth 30–40mm long, ± 10mm wide.

Common names refer to the peculiar growth habit of the plants; older plants in the centre of a clump die back, with the younger ones remaining in a circle on the periphery, thus forming a ring or *kraal*.

BEN-ERIK VAN WYK

Aloe davyana (= *A. greatheadii* var. *davyana*)

Asphodelaceae
Winter

E Common spotted aloe **A** Gewone bontaalwyn

Stemless succulent with leaves in a basal rosette; occurring in grassland and bushveld, often in stony places. Leaves with upper surface green and dotted with many whitish spots, lower surface whitish green and ± without spots; margin with sharp, brown spines. Inflorescence up to 1m high, with up to five branches; racemes ± densely congested, conical, 150–200mm long; flowers with perianth usually pale pink, constricted above the ovary.

Plants tend to proliferate in overgrazed areas. An effective soil binder that can be used to stabilise soil banks and disturbed areas. Leaf pulp used medicinally to treat burns, sores and wounds. *A. greatheadii* has shorter racemes (± 90mm). *A. transvaalensis*, a summer-flowering species, has reddish flowers in well-spaced racemes.

Aloe maculata (= *A. saponaria*)
E Soap aloe **A** Seepaalwyn

Asphodelaceae
Summer–Spring

Succulent that has leaves in a rather open, flat, basal rosette; stemless, or with a short, erect stem less than 1m high; occurring in coastal and montane grassland, usually in large colonies; solitary or in clumps of several individuals. Leaves spotted above and below; tip dry, twisted; margin with brown teeth. Inflorescence with up to six branches; flowers in dense, flat-topped racemes, yellow, orange or red.

A widespread and variable species; however, the usually flat-topped racemes are very characteristic, making this one of the easier spotted-leaved aloes to identify. Widely used in traditional medicine to treat wounds and other ailments. Leaf sap formerly used in the tanning of hides. Cut leaves yield a copious flow of sap, which froths like soap when the cut ends are rubbed together, hence the common names.

TOM DE WAAL

Aloe striata
E Coral aloe **A** Gladdeblaaraalwyn

Asphodelaceae
Winter–Spring

Succulent that has leaves in a basal rosette, stemless, or with a short, creeping stem; occurring in thicket and karroid vegetation, usually in large colonies. Leaves pale blue-green, often tinged with red, distinctly striate, unspotted; margin spineless, with a soft, reddish edge. Inflorescence a branched, flat-topped raceme, up to 1m high; buds and flowers coral-red, ± drooping; perianth 25–35mm long, with a basal swelling.

One of the very few species of aloe with spineless leaves. An attractive garden plant. A cross with *A. maculata* is probably the most widely cultivated aloe hybrid (hybrid retains pink marginal border). Related to *A. karasbergensis* (Northern Cape and southern Namibia), which has conspicuously green-veined leaves and a much-branched, pyramidal panicle.

*Campuloclinium macrocephalum

E Pompom weed **A** Pompombossie

Asteraceae

Summer–Autumn

Erect perennial herb up to 1.3m high, covered with rough hairs throughout, with a woody rootstock; occurring in grassland and bushveld, often forming dense stands, especially in vleis and old cultivated fields. Leaves oblanceolate, tapering to a stalk-like base; margin toothed. Flower heads (see page 142) discoid, fluffy, arranged in a compound inflorescence, bright pink-purple.

A declared weed invading grassland and bushveld in many parts of the region; originally from South America. It displaces native species and reduces the biological diversity and carrying capacity of the veld. Started to spread noticeably in Gauteng in the late 1980s. Individual plants produce large quantities of wind-dispersed seed. A stem- and leaf-feeding thrips (*Liothrips tractabilis*) has been released as part of a biological control campaign intended to decrease the number of flowers and, ultimately, seeds produced by the weed.

Cosmos bipinnatus (= *Bidens formosa*)

E Cosmos **A** Kosmos

Asteraceae

Autumn

Bushy annual herb, up to 2m high; occurring mainly in grassland, usually in dense stands along roadsides, in cultivated lands and in other disturbed places. Leaves opposite, stalked and stem-clasping; blade deeply and finely divided. Flower heads radiate (see page 142); ray florets red, pink or white; disc florets yellow.

A native of the southern USA and Mexico. Introduced to South Africa with animal fodder in the late 1890s. First recorded as a naturalised weed near Pretoria in 1904, only reaching KwaZulu-Natal in 1945. Now well established throughout the cool and wet parts of the Highveld, where mass blooming of plants creates spectacular flower displays in autumn. The proportion of white, pink and red flowers varies from place to place. Generic name from the Greek *kosmos* = beautiful.

Gerbera jamesonii

E Barberton daisy   **A** Barbertonse madeliefie

Asteraceae
Spring–Summer

Stemless herb with a perennial rootstock; occurring in bushveld, often in semishade. Leaves with margin unevenly and deeply lobed and toothed. Flower heads radiate (see page 142), ± 80mm in diameter; ray florets usually deep orange-red to red; disc florets yellow to orange.

Probably the best-known contribution to horticulture to come from the South African bushveld; gerbera cultivars, in a rich variety of colours, are popular garden plants and cut flowers throughout the world. Most were derived from hybrids made by a British nurseryman, Richard Irwin Lynch, in about 1890. About 15 species of *Gerbera* occur in the region. *G. aurantiaca* has bright orange-red ray florets, disc florets with black anthers and leaves that are ± smooth. It occurs in grassland, mainly in KwaZulu-Natal.

Helichrysum adenocarpum

E Pink everlasting   **A** Pienksewejaartjie

Asteraceae
Summer

Herb up to 450mm high with a perennial rootstock; occurring in grassland, often in large colonies on moist slopes. Leaves in one to several rosettes, basal ones ± flat on the ground, 20–40 × 15–25mm, grey, woolly, ± prostrate. Flowering stems emerging from the side of rosettes, erect, simple or branching above, covered by smaller, narrow, woolly leaves; flower heads (see page 142) 15–20mm long, 25–35mm in diameter, bracts glossy, white, or white tipped with pink, crimson or scarlet; centre yellow, often tipped red.

Heads open fully only in bright sunlight, close toward evening. Dried flower heads retain their colour; used in dried-flower arrangements. In *H. monticola* the flowering stems emerge from the centre of the leaf rosettes; found mainly in the Drakensberg Escarpment and foothills.

PETER WARREN –ISPOT

Helichrysum ecklonis

E Giant pink everlasting **A** Reusepienksewejaartjie

Asteraceae
Spring–Summer

Herb up to 500mm high, with a perennial rootstock; occurring in grassland, usually as isolated tufts. Leaves in one to several rosettes, basal ones ± flat on the ground, up to 200 × 20mm, loosely covered in woolly grey hairs, especially on the lower surface. Flowering stems emerging from the centre of rosettes, erect, unbranched, covered by smaller, narrow, woolly leaves; flower heads (see page 142) 25–30mm long, ± 55mm in diameter; bracts glossy, white to deep rose-pink; centre yellow.

Flower heads used in dried-flower arrangements. Named after the plant collector. Christian Ecklon (1795–1868). *H. vernum*, from the high Drakensberg between KwaZulu-Natal and Lesotho, has similar flower heads, but this species forms dense mats.

Phaenocoma prolifera

E Pink Cape everlasting **A** Rooisewejaartjie

Asteraceae
Summer

Rigid, evergreen, much-branched perennial shrublet, up to 600mm high; occurring in fynbos on sandy, acidic soils, often on rocky coastal mountain slopes and along roadsides. Stems covered with dense, short wool. Leaves very small and scale-like, crowded on short side branches, greyish green. Flower heads (see page 142) large and showy; bracts numerous, glossy, deep pink, fading pale pink to whitish; centre white.

Plants are aromatic and harsh, hence they are not browsed by animals. Flower heads used in dried-flower arrangements. Old flower heads may remain on the plant for many months. The only member of the genus. *Edmondia pinifolia*, a pink everlasting from the same general area, has ± unbranched stems and flower heads with a yellow centre.

Senecio elegans
E Purple senecio **A** Strandblommetjie

Asteraceae
Spring

Robust, bushy annual, up to 600mm high; occurring in strandveld and fynbos, often on coastal sand dunes. Stems with rough hairs. Leaves deeply once or twice divided and ± curly, with rough hairs, often ± sticky; margins rolled under. Flower heads (see page 142) in branched, flat-topped inflorescences, ± 25mm in diameter; ray florets 12–14, magenta; disc florets yellow; base of head globose, involucral bracts in a single row, hairless, black-tipped.

Plants near the seashore tend to have more fleshy leaves. An attractive annual for the garden; sow seed in March. Unpalatable to livestock. *S. arenarius*, also with bicoloured heads, is a more slender plant with the base of the flower head cylindrical, hairy, with 1–3 small involucral bracts. It is part of the floral display in Namaqualand.

Senecio speciosus
E Beautiful senecio **A** Pienk-senecio

Asteraceae
Spring

Perennial herb with a stout, woody rootstock; occurring in grassland and fynbos, usually in moist places. Leaves mainly in a basal rosette, spatulate or elliptic, ± 100–200 × 20–40mm, usually with sticky (glandular) hairs; base tapering, broad, flat and stalk-like, stem-clasping; margin pinnately lobed, margin of lobes often toothed. Several flowering stems form from the same crown, often slightly reclining at the base, then erect, branched above; flower heads (see page 142) ± 12–15mm in diameter; ray florets 14–18, they and the disc florets are pink to purple.

Used in traditional medicine for various ailments. Attractive plant for frost-free gardens. *S. macrocephalus*, also with similar-coloured disc and ray florets, has ± stalkless leaves with the margin often ± smooth or very shallowly toothed.

*Zinnia peruviana

E Redstar zinnia **A** Wildejakobregop

Asteraceae

Summer–Autumn

Slender, erect annual herb, up to 500mm high; occurring in grassland and bushveld, often in disturbed or shady places. Leaves stalkless, opposite, widely spaced, covered with rough hairs. Flowers heads (see page 142) solitary, at the ends of stalks, which gradually thicken toward the head; ray florets red or pale orange, persistent, drying to purplish brown; centre conical, brownish or yellow.

A native of South America, now naturalised in many parts of the world. Not a serious weed in agricultural land. The genus contains ± 11 species, some of which were already grown by the Aztecs. Cultivars of the Mexican *Z. violacea* are popular garden ornamentals (zinnias); they come in all colours, except blue. The generic name honours Johann Gottfried Zinn (1727–1759), a German professor of botany at Gottingen.

Impatiens sylvicola

E Forest impatiens **A** Bos-impatiens

Balsaminaceae

Summer

Soft, erect, herbaceous annual or perennial, up to 400mm high; occurring in damp, shady places in forest, often in forest clearings or along forest paths and roads. Leaves broadly ovate to ± elliptic; margin finely and bluntly toothed; stalk up to 35mm long. Flowers irregular, pink or purplish pink with a deep mauve or reddish blotch toward the base of the two upper side petals; one of the sepals spurred.

Plants often occur in dense stands. The fleshy fruits open explosively to scatter the seed; this response can be triggered by gently squeezing the tip of a ripe capsule. *I. hochstetteri* is another common forest species in the region. It has a paler pink flower with the two lower (front) petals narrower and the two upper side ones larger. Several species grown as garden and house plants.

Hermannia grandiflora

E Bell bush **A** Ouma-se-kappie

Byttneriaceae
Summer–Autumn

Much-branched perennial shrublet, with a roundish shape, up to 1m high; occurring in karroid vegetation. Leaves alternate or in tufts, elliptic, 2–15 × 2–4mm; margin coarsely toothed. Flowers borne in groups of two on long, slender stalks near branch tips, all facing downward; petals five, free, pale red, twisted.

Flowers are usually produced in profusion and may cover the whole bush, resulting in striking patches of colour. Drought-resistant, palatable and well grazed by livestock; presence of plants indicates veld in good condition. Superficially very similar to *H. stricta*, which also produces red flowers in profusion. It has larger, solitary flowers on stalks rarely longer than 12mm, and has a more restricted distribution in the hot, arid areas along the lower reaches of the Orange River.

**Canna indica*

E Wild canna **A** Wildekanna

Cannaceae
Summer–Autumn

Perennial herb, up to 1.5m high, with annual stems from a swollen tuberous rhizome; occurring in moist grassland and along forest margins. Leaves large, broad, pinnately veined with a distinct midrib; stalk present, sheathing the stem. Flowers in racemes at the ends of erect stems; sepals and petals three each, green; showy part of flowers formed by sterile, petal-like, red stamens, the largest of these being orange-red, reflexed and rolled back on itself. Fruit a warty capsule.

Black seeds used as beads. The genus is native to Central America and the West Indies. Several cultivars are grown as greenhouse and garden ornamentals; many developed from *C. indica*. *C. edulis* is of considerable economic importance as the source of a starch known as purple or Queensland arrowroot.

Gloriosa superba
🇪 Flame lily 🇦 Vlamlelie

Colchicaceae
Summer

Perennial herb with climbing annual shoots from an underground tuber; occurring in thicket, along forest margins and on coastal dunes. Leaves strap-shaped, tapering to a coiled tendril, glossy green. Flowers large and conspicuous, downward-facing; petals strongly reflexed, yellow, red-and-yellow, red or deep pink, margin undulate; style bent at a right angle to the ovary. Capsules green, with bright red seed.

Plants show great variety in flower size and colour. Plants poisonous, containing colchicine and related compounds. Colchicine has anticancer properties, but is too toxic for human use. Widely utilised in traditional medicine, but such practices should be discouraged, because the plant is implicated in human deaths and developmental abnormalities in newborn babies.

Ipomoea crassipes
🇪 Leafy-flowered ipomoea 🇦 Pienkpatat

Convolvulaceae
Spring–Summer

Herb with trailing or ± erect annual stems from a perennial tuberous rootstock; occurring mainly in grassland. Leaves very variable, usually ovate to lanceolate, 15–80 × 8–30mm, hairy, often with a purplish margin; stalk up to 10mm long. Flowers solitary; calyx surrounded by leaf-like bracts; corolla funnel-shaped, 35–60mm in diameter, magenta or pale mauve, rarely white with a dark purple centre. Fruit a dehiscent capsule, ± 10mm in diameter.

Very variable in leaf shape and habit, but the presence of leaf-like bracts below the calyx is diagnostic. Tuber used medicinally against dysentery, sores and hiccups; it is also said to be edible. About 50 species of *Ipomoea* are native to the region. *I. batatas*, originally from Central America, is the cultivated sweet potato.

Ipomoea ommaneyi

E Silver-leaved ipomoea **A** Beespatat

Convolvulaceae
Summer

Prostrate perennial herb; tuber very large (at least 1 × 0.3m), with robust (up to 10mm in diameter), annual trailing stems; occurring in grassland and bushveld. Leaves all pointing upward, ovate-lanceolate or oblong-lanceolate, very large (up to 300 × 120mm), both surfaces sparsely covered with silvery white hairs; margin wavy with a dense fringe of yellowish hairs. Flowers clustered together in dense heads on erect stalks; corolla funnel-shaped, rose-magenta, with distinct midpetaline areas that are white and densely silky outside.

Most readily noticed by its robust trailing stems and large, silvery leaves. Formerly crushed dried tubers were mixed with curdled milk or with water and used as a famine food. Grazed by livestock. Larger tubers may be centuries old.

Ipomoea pes-caprae

E Dune morning glory **A** Duinpatat

Convolvulaceae
Summer–Autumn

Perennial herb, with long-trailing stems rooting at the nodes, sprouting from a tuberous rootstock; milky latex present; occurring on sandy beaches. Leaves rounded and ± two-lobed, thick and leathery, up to 100mm in diameter, hairless; stalk usually up to 120mm long. Flowers solitary or in clusters on a stout erect stalk; corolla funnel-shaped, ± 60mm in diameter, pink, magenta or purple, darker inside at the base.

Common pioneer (sand-binder) on tropical beaches; usually growing just above the high-water mark. Midrib below with two glands (extrafloral nectaries) at the leaf base; these attract nectar-feeding insects (including ants), most probably for protection. Tuber, leaves and seed used medicinally; leaves show anti-inflammatory activity. Specific name means 'like a goat's foot', and refers to the shape of the leaves.

TONY ABBOTT

Turbina oblongata (= *Ipomoea oblongata*)

Convolvulaceae

E Grassland turbina   **A** Grasveldvalspatat

Summer

Perennial herb, with annual prostrate stems from a large tuber; occurring in grassland and bushveld. Leaves with short stalks, ± erect, usually ovate or elliptic, 20–100 × 15–50mm, upper surface sparsely and lower surface sparsely or densely covered with yellowish hairs; margin ± wavy with a fringe of hairs. Flowers usually solitary, on erect stalks; outer sepals ± densely covered with stiff, yellowish hairs; corolla funnel-shaped, ± 60mm in diameter, magenta.

In large plants the tubers may be well over a century old; seeds are rarely produced. Tuber and leaves used in traditional medicine. *Turbina* and *Ipomoea* are very similar in vegetative and floral characters. They differ primarily in their capsular fruit; those of the former being indehiscent, the latter dehiscent by four, rarely six valves.

BRAAM VAN WYK & SASA MALAN

Turbina oenotheroides (= *Ipomoea oenotheroides*)

Convolvulaceae

E Christmas flower   **A** Krismisblom

Summer

Erect, much-branched shrublet, up to 1m high, sprouting from perennial tuberous roots; occurring in grassland and karroid vegetation, often along roadsides. Leaves linear to lanceolate, usually 3–6 × 2–8mm; stalk usually up to 6mm long. Flowers solitary on slender stalks in leaf axils; corolla funnel-shaped, 35–70mm in diameter, bright magenta or magenta-pink, midpetaline areas usually densely covered with short, appressed, silvery hairs.

Plants tend to grow in large colonies. They flower around Christmas, hence the common names. Flowers open after sunrise, fade by midday. They are fed on by yellow-and-black CMR beetles (*Mylabris oculata*), which consume the corolla as soon as it opens in the morning. The tuber is said to be inedible.

Cotyledon orbiculata
🇪 Pig's ears 🇦 Plakkie

Crassulaceae
Winter–Spring

Robust perennial succulent, with erect or reclining stems with the tips growing upward; occurring in karroid vegetation, thicket, bushveld and rocky places in grassland. Leaves very variable in shape, usually ± flattened, greyish green, with a white powdery bloom; margin reddish. Flowers in compact clusters at the end of a sturdy, erect stalk, pendulous; corolla ± cylindrical with recurved lobes, orange or pinkish red.

Pollinated mainly by honeybees. The leaves, applied as a dressing, are a popular and effective traditional remedy to treat corns and warts. Plants are toxic because of the presence of several cardiac glycosides of the bufadienolide type; cause *krimpsiekte* in domestic animals especially sheep and goats. Poisoning may be acute or chronic, the latter due to the cumulative effect of the toxin.

BRAAM VAN WYK & SASA MALAN

Crassula perfoliata (= *C. falcata*)
🇪 Flat-leaved crassula 🇦 Platblaarplakkie

Crassulaceae
Autumn–Spring

Evergreen, erect, little-branched succulent up to 1.5m high; occurring in thicket or rocky places in grassland. Stems are covered with coarse, ± rounded papillae. Leaves opposite or ± in a fan, very variable, ± finger-like, flat or laterally compressed, 40–120 × 12–35mm, green to grey, densely covered with coarse, rounded, erect papillae. Flowers numerous, congested in a rounded, flat-topped inflorescence at the end of an erect stalk, the latter with reduced leaves; corolla tubular, fused basally for 1–1.5mm, white, pink to scarlet, lobes 3–6mm long; stamens with black anthers.

This is a variable species with a number of distinct forms; var. *minor*, with laterally flattened leaves, is illustrated here. A handsome plant that does well in dry rockeries.

Erica cerinthoides

E Fire heath **A** Rooihaartjie

Ericaceae

All year

Erect shrublet, up to 500mm high, sprouting from a perennial rootstock; occurring in fynbos and grassland, often in rocky places. Leaves in clusters, needle-like, glandular. Flowers in clusters at ends of branches; corolla tubular, usually 25–35mm long (± 12mm in var. *barbertona*), dark pinkish red or rarely white tipped with red, with spreading hairs; anthers without appendages.

Most widespread erica in the region, and one of a mere handful that occurs in the summer-rainfall area. Flowering is stimulated by fire. *Erica* derives from the Greek *ereike*, a name used for a heath by Pliny and Theophrastus. More than 760 of some 860 *Erica* species found worldwide occur in the region. Of these, about 730 occur in the Cape Floristic Kingdom, making it the most species-rich genus in the country.

Erica mammosa

E Nipple heath **A** Rooiklossieheide

Ericaceae

Summer–Autumn

Slender, erect shrublet up to 1.8m high; occurring in fynbos, often in sandy seepage areas. Leaves needle-like, overlapping. Flowers in loose spikes near ends of branches, drooping; corolla tubular, slightly puffed, 24–26mm long, usually bright red, but also white, orange, pink, purple or green, with four indents at the base of the tube; anthers with tail-like appendages.

A hardy species occasionally grown in gardens, even in areas with winter frost. Like most ericas it requires a sunny position and well-drained, acidic, sandy soil that is rich in humus. All ericas have roots with special fungal associates (mycorrhizas). The specific name is from the Latin *mammosus* = with breasts; presumably referring to the shape of the flowers, which resemble a cow's teats.

Erica plukenetii

E Plukenet's heath **A** Hangertjie

Ericaceae
All year

Erect shrublet, with ± feathery foliage, up to 1m high; hairless; occurring in fynbos, on mountain slopes and flats. Leaves arranged in successive whorls on the branches, needle-like, usually 12–16mm long. Flowers in densely packed spikes, usually some distance below the tips of shoots, drooping; corolla tubular and inflated, 13–18mm long, pink, reddish purple, red-orange or sometimes white with green lobes; anthers positioned at tip of filaments, long (up to 12mm) and narrow, brownish, projecting conspicuously far beyond the corolla tube, without tail-like appendages.

Flowers pollinated by sunbirds. Similar to *E. coccinea*, which has shorter leaves (4–8mm) arranged in tufts, and a whorl of sepal-like bracts below and partly overlapping with the calyx.

Erica pulchella

E Pink-spike heath **A** Pienkaarheide

Ericaceae
Spring–Autumn

Floriferous, bushy perennial herb with many erect stems, up to 600mm high; occurring in fynbos, often in dense stands on dry sandy flats and lower mountain slopes. Leaves needle-like, pointing toward tips of stems. Flowers in leaf axils toward ends of branches, often in a spike-like formation; corolla bell-shaped, 3–4mm long, lobes slightly spreading, pale pink to dark red, occasionally white; anthers do not protrude from the corolla, each one has two slender, tail-like appendages at the base.

Very variable as to flower colour and flowering time. Young plants tend to be more floriferous than the older ones. Very similar to *E. longiaristata* from the Bredasdorp District, a more spreading and lax shrublet with flowers that have a slightly wider mouth.

COLIN PATERSON-JONES

Erica sparsa (= *E. floribunda*)

Ericaceae
Winter–Spring

E Pink-smoke heath **A** Kerker

Floriferous, bushy perennial shrublet, up to 1m high; occurring mainly in fynbos and grassy fynbos, often in dense colonies on hillsides and in clearings. Leaves small and needle-like. Flowers very small, produced in masses along stems, usually completely concealing the leaves; calyx short, pink or, rarely, white; corolla cup-shaped with an open mouth, ± 1mm long, pale pink or, rarely, white; anthers dark purple, not protruding, without tail-like appendages; style protruding, pink.

The Afrikaans common name is said to be onomatopoeic, being a representation of the harsh, grating noise that is produced when one walks through the plants, or when the wheels of a cart ride over them. This plant is very common in the Tsitsikamma area, especially along roadsides.

JUDD KIRKEL

Erica versicolor

Ericaceae
Winter–Spring

E Tall sticky heath **A** Groottaaiheide

Sturdy shrub, up to 3m high, with branches straight or variously curved; occurring in fynbos, usually on lower mountain slopes and along roadsides. Leaves small, needle-like. Flowers clustered at the ends of branches; corolla tubular, 22–28mm long, usually with a red base and a greenish to white tip, very sticky; stamens included; anthers borne on the side of each filament, without tail-like appendages.

The flowers are pollinated by sunbirds. Glossy outer appearance of the corolla is due to a very sticky secretion that probably serves to deter non-pollinating nectar-eating insects. This is supported by the observation that insects are often seen trapped on the corolla, as if caught on flypaper. Sticky corollas are found in several native heath species.

Indigofera heterophylla
🇪 Lucerne bush 🇦 Boontjiekaroo

Fabaceae
Spring

Prostrate perennial shrublet, up to 300mm high, often scrambling over other plants; occurring in fynbos, grassland and karroid vegetation, often in rocky places. Leaves trifoliolate; leaflets ±10 × 5mm, dark green; stalk up to 15mm long. Flowers (see page 142) in short, erect racemes at the ends of stems, bright pink to brick red. Pods cylindrical, ± 20mm long.

A valuable grazing bush that is highly palatable to livestock; one of the first species to disappear from overgrazed veld. Leaves are reminiscent of those of lucerne, hence the English common name. About 200 species of *Indigofera* are native to the region. Those from the Cape Floristic Kingdom tend to have more pinkish flowers, whereas those with reddish flowers tend to predominate in other areas where these plants occur.

JUDD KIRKEL

Indigofera hilaris
🇪 Grassland indigofera 🇦 Grasveld-indigofera

Fabaceae
Spring

Perennial shrublet with erect, sparsely branched stems from a woody tuber; occurring in grassland. Stems with non-glandular, appressed hairs. Leaves pinnately compound, greyish green; leaflets five, two opposite pairs with a terminal one. Flowers (see page 142) in axillary racemes, which are often shorter than the leaves, pink to reddish pink.

Flowers profusely after fire. One of the typical pre-rain flowers in the Grassland Biome. The generic name comes from indigo, the blue dye (Greek: *indicos* = of India, whence the dye originally comes) and *fero*, to produce. The dye is primarily obtained from *I. tinctoria* (Southeast Asia) and *I. dimidiata* (called *I. arrecta* in southern Africa). Branches are subjected to a rather complicated fermentation process. Today, however, the dye is produced synthetically.

Indigofera sanguinea

E Blood-red indigofera **A** Bloedrooi-indigofera

Fabaceae
Spring–Summer

Spreading perennial shrublet with erect shoots, up to 600mm high, sprouting annually from a tuberous rootstock; occurring in grassland, often in rocky places. Leaves pinnately compound; leaflets ± seven pairs, ± 10 × 7mm each. Flowers (see page 142) in dense, erect racemes, bright orange-red. Pods cylindrical, ± 40 × 2mm, hairy.

Indigofera flowers have evolved a fascinating, explosive pollen-presentation mechanism. In the newly opened flower the stamen tube is held under tension between the keel petals by projections on their upper edges. The pressure exerted by a visiting bee dislodges these projections, releasing the stamen tube and style, which spring up, forcefully striking the underside of the visitor. Once 'exploded', the spent flower hangs limply open.

Pseudarthria hookeri

E Velvet bean **A** Fluweelboontjie

Fabaceae
Summer–Autumn

Robust, sparsely branched, erect perennial, up to 3m high, sprouting annually from a woody rootstock; occurring on forest margins, in associated grassland and in bushveld, often along roadsides. Stems angular, velvety. Leaves trifoliolate; leaflets ± 70 × 40mm, dark green with rough hairs above, whitish green with dense hairs below. Flowers (see page 142) in large terminal panicles, bright pink. Pods 12–38 × 3–4 mm, velvety.

Plants often appear top-heavy and bend down under the weight of the large inflorescences. Curled hairs on the leaves enable them to stick to clothing. The hairy pods adhere to passing objects. Leafy branches are used to catch bedbugs; placed around a sleeping person at night, the bugs are said to be trapped between the dense hairs on the leaves and stems.

Sphenostylis angustifolia

E Wild sweetpea **A** Wilde-ertjie

Fabaceae
Spring–Summer

Perennial shrublet with spreading to erect annual stems from a woody rootstock, up to 400mm high; occurring in grassland, especially in rocky places. Leaves trifoliolate, with stalk 20–80mm long; leaflets ± 40 × 5–10mm. Flowers (see page 142) 1–4 at the end of an erect inflorescence stalk; corolla bright pink with a yellow blotch on the standard petal, rarely white fading to cream, keel twisted.

Flowering is stimulated by late winter fires. Deflection of the keel and style to one side is known as enantiostyly or enantiomorphy; flowers may be either left- or right-handed, depending on the plant. The stylar deflection results in pollen deposition on one side of the bee's abdomen, and is a special adaptation to facilitate cross-pollination and outcrossing. Leaf infusions used in traditional medicine.

BRAAM VAN WYK & SASA MALAN

Sutherlandia frutescens (= *Lessertia frutescens*)

E Cancer bush **A** Kankerbos

Fabaceae
Spring–Summer

Short-lived perennial shrublet, up to 1m high; occurring in fynbos and karroid vegetation, often along roadsides. Leaves pinnately compound with numerous small leaflets, silvery grey due to a dense cover of silvery hairs. Flowers (see page 142) in clusters, bright red. Pods inflated, papery, reddish-tinged when young.

Flowers pollinated by sunbirds; seed dispersed when pods are blown around by wind. A popular traditional remedy (extremely bitter-tasting) for a variety of ailments, including colds, influenza, diabetes, varicose veins, liver problems and cancer. Plants are very palatable to livestock and of high nutritional value; may give milk a bitter taste. The species of *Sutherlandia* (about six) are all very similar-looking and difficult to tell apart. Members of the group contain anticancer compounds.

Tephrosia grandiflora

E Large pink tephrosia **A** Grootpienk-tephrosia

Fabaceae

All year

Erect annual or short-lived perennial shrublet, up to 1.5m high; occurring in bushveld and grassland. Leaflets 3–5 pairs, ± 15 × 6mm, with fine silvery grey hairs below; stipules narrowly ovate, ± 10–32mm long, longer than wide. Flowers (see page 142) pea-like, clustered in terminal racemes, large (± 20mm long), bright magenta-pink. Pods ± 30 × 8mm, many-seeded.

Attractive garden plant. Root infusions used to treat chest ailments. Like other members of the genus the plant contains tephrosin, rotenone and related compounds that have strong insecticidal and piscicidal properties. Pounded leaves, pods or roots thrown into a pool suffocate fish, thus paralysing them so that they can easily be caught. Fish so poisoned can be eaten without ill effect.

TREVOR COLEMAN

Chironia baccifera

E Christmas berry **A** Aambeibossie

Gentianaceae

Spring

Evergreen, rounded, much-branched perennial shrublet, up to 1m high; occurring in fynbos, grassland, and especially coastal dune vegetation. Stems angular or narrowly winged. Leaves inconspicuous, stalkless, thin to ± fleshy, 5–20 × 1–3mm; margin rolled downward. Flowers ± solitary, scattered all over bush, pink; anthers yellow. Fruit berry-like, produced in abundance, bright red, drying black.

A popular traditional medicine; extensively used as a blood purifier to treat skin problems, boils and haemorrhoids. Infusions are bitter-tasting and have a strong purgative action; also used as an external application. The plant is said to be potentially toxic and it should only be taken internally when administered by a knowledgeable person. Plants are easily propagated from seed, but they are frost-sensitive.

Chironia palustris

E Marsh chironia **A** Bitterwortel

Gentianaceae
Spring–Summer

Erect, bushy perennial herb, up to 700mm high; occurring in grassland, often forming dense clumps in marshy places and along stream banks. Leaves initially in a basal rosette, blue-green, ± succulent. Flowers in well-spaced terminal groups, ± 25mm in diameter, bright rose-pink; calyx ± as long as corolla tube; anthers slightly twisted; buds with calyx lobes and bracts not tapering into a long, slender point.

Calyx lobes sometimes ± sticky and function as extrafloral nectaries attracting ants. Root used medicinally to treat colic and diarrhoea; plants may be poisonous. About 15 species of *Chironia* are native to South Africa. *C. purpurascens* (with ± the same range) has deep magenta-pink flowers, calyx lobes longer than the corolla tube and buds with calyx lobes and bracts tapering to a long point.

Pelargonium cucullatum

E Hooded-leaf pelargonium **A** Wildemalva

Geraniaceae
Spring

Sturdy, bushy perennial shrublet, up to 2m high; occurring in fynbos, usually in dense stands in coastal areas. Woody at the base, young stems ± herbaceous. Leaves ± kidney-shaped, pleated, up to 45–60mm, sometimes ± cup-shaped (hooded), with long, soft hairs; margin irregularly toothed, often reddish. Flowers in hollow-stalked umbels, each with 4–10 flowers; petals five, pink-purple to dark purple, upper two petals slightly larger, with dark red veins; faintly scented.

All parts emit a strong scent when crushed. Root and leaves formerly used medicinally. Introduced into cultivation in England in 1690, it is the main ancestor of the popular Regal pelargoniums of horticulture. Stem cuttings are quick-and-easy to root. Leaf and root extensively used in traditional medicine.

Pelargonium incrassatum
E Namaqualand beauty **A** T'knytjie

Geraniaceae

Spring

Perennial herb, up to 300mm high with a turnip-shaped tuber; occurring in karroid vegetation, usually among granitic rocks. Leaves in a basal rosette, ovate to narrowly ovate in outline, deeply lobed into scalloped segments, with silvery hairs. Flowers in an umbel at the end of a long, erect, unbranched stalk; petals five, bright pinkish purple, upper two much larger than the rest.

The brilliantly coloured flowers can be spotted from afar among the colourful spring-flowering annuals of Namaqualand; pollinated by *Prosoeca peringueyi*, a long-tongued fly. Plants are deciduous during the dry season (summer). Peeled tubers cooked in milk or baked under hot ash are considered a delicacy by the local people. An attractive pot plant; plants should be kept dry during the dormant season.

Pelargonium luridum
E Stalk-flowered pelargonium **A** Grasveld-rabas

Geraniaceae

Spring–Summer

Perennial herb, up to 1m high, with a tuber; occurring in grassland and bushveld. Leaves in a basal rosette, usually covered with long hairs, extremely variable, even on the same plant; lamina varies from slightly lobed to deeply dissected, the segments thread-like in some forms. Flowers in an umbel of 5–60 flowers at the end of a long, slender, erect, unbranched stalk; petals five, ± equal and without blotches, very variable in colour; white, cream, creamy pale green, salmon pink or greenish yellow.

A conspicuous species because of its tall inflorescences that sway in the slightest breeze above the grasses. An infusion of the tuber, which is pinkish red inside, is a popular traditional remedy against diarrhoea and dysentery; pharmacological effects may be due to the presence of tannins.

BRAAM VAN WYK & SASA MALAN

Pelargonium peltatum
E Ivy-leaved pelargonium   **A** Kolsuring

Herbaceous, ± hairless perennial creeper; occurring in thicket and along forest margins. Leaves ± rounded in outline, bluntly five-angled or lobed, ± shield-shaped with the stalk attached slightly to the inside of the margin (peltate), or cordate with stalk inserted at the margin (*P. lateripes*), sometimes with a dark reddish marking centrally on the upper surface; margin smooth. Flowers in stalked umbels of 2–9 flowers; petals five, mauve or pinkish mauve to pale pink, upper two slightly larger with darker markings; sepals often tinged dull red.

Leaves with a sour-tasting sap used as an antiseptic for sore throats. Petals yield a blue pigment once used in paintings. The ancestor of many cultivars of 'ivy-leaved geraniums' grown in gardens worldwide; introduced to Holland in 1700 and Britain in 1774.

Veltheimia capensis
E Sand lily   **A** Sandlelie

Erect perennial with a partly exposed bulb; occurring in karroid vegetation, fynbos and strandveld. Leaves in a basal rosette, spreading, greyish green, hairless; margin usually undulate. Flowers in a dense raceme at the end of a sturdy, spotted, erect stalk, drooping, cylindrical, various shades of mottled pink, tipped green; stamens exserted a short way from mouth of tube. Fruit a capsule, large, membranous, with pear-shaped black seed.

Easily grown in gardens, but frost-sensitive; requires sandy soil, a sunny position and dry conditions when dormant in summer. Bulbs should be planted with at least one-third above ground. *V. bracteata* (mainly Eastern Cape) is the only other member of the genus. It is ± evergreen and prefers shady conditions; bulb is completely below ground.

Rhodohypoxis baurii
E Red star **A** Rooisterretjie

Hypoxidaceae
Spring–Summer

Small perennial herb, up to 150mm high, with a tuberous rhizome; occurring in grassland, usually in damp and rocky places. Leaves spreading, sparsely covered with long hairs. Flowers on long, slender stalks; perianth with three large and three small, ± horizontally spreading lobes, usually pink, red or white, faintly scented; anthers hidden by the upward bending of the three inner perianth lobes.

The most widespread member of the genus; floral colour very variable, even in the same colony. Plants often grow in dense stands, creating colourful patches. Attractive garden plant, best suited for areas with a cool, moist climate. *R. milloides* has hairless leaves, or very nearly so. There are ± six species of *Rhodohypoxis*, all confined to the central Drakensberg and surrounding areas.

Antholyza ringens (= *Babiana ringens*)
E Rat's tail **A** Rotstert

Iridaceae
Winter–Spring

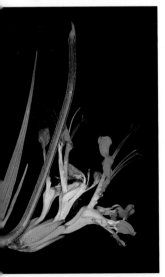

Erect perennial, up to 400mm high, with a deep-seated corm; occurring mainly in fynbos and strandveld, often in sandy soil. Leaves stiff and erect, strongly pleated. Flowers on a ± horizontal side branch toward base of main inflorescence axis, irregular; perianth strongly two-lipped, with protruding stamens held within a tube formed by the upper lip, bright red.

Flowers conspicuous and can be seen from a distance; pollinated by sunbirds. Upper part of main inflorescence axis remains sterile and bare, hence the common names. As with several local members of the Iridaceae the corms, known as *uintjies*, are edible; they are used in a variety of dishes. *A. plicata* (= *Babiana thunbergii*) from Namaqualand grows up to 1m high, and the inflorescence has several side branches.

Crocosmia paniculata (= *Curtonus paniculatus*)

E Pleated leaves **A** Waaierlelie

Iridaceae
Summer

Robust perennial, up to 2.5m high, sprouting annually from a corm; occurring as dense stands in grassland, usually in marshy places and where water collects along roadsides. Leaves in a fan, stiff, erect, deeply pleated, ± 800 × 60mm. Flowers borne well above the leaves, arranged on several well-spaced, horizontally spreading and ± zigzagged side branches toward the end of a tall, erect flowering stalk; corolla tubular, strongly two-lipped with protruding stamens, dark brick red.

Flowers pollinated by sunbirds, which use the sturdy side branches of the inflorescence as perches. As in many bird-pollinated flowers, they are scentless; birds generally have a poorly developed sense of smell. Used in traditional medicine. Attractive, cold-hardy garden plant; dormant during winter.

Dierama spp.

E Hairbells **A** Grasklokkies

Iridaceae
Mainly Spring–Summer

Evergreen, grass-like perennial herbs with corms; occurring in grassland. Flowers borne on tall, slender stems that divide at the top into a number of usually pendulous flowering branchlets on thin, wiry, flexible stalks; perianth bell-shaped, very dark red to pale yellow or whitish, but most often shades of pink or mauve, each perianth lobe (tepal) usually marked with a ± diamond-shaped 'eye' inside at the base.

The slender inflorescences sway in the slightest breeze. About 37 species of *Dierama* occur in the region; distribution map shows total range of the genus. Correct species identification often requires expert knowledge, the morphology of the bracts being of great importance. Accompanying photograph is of *D. latifolium*, a species from KwaZulu-Natal and the Eastern Cape.

Gladiolus oppositiflorus

Iridaceae

E Salmon gladiolus **A** Transkeiswaardlelie

Summer

Erect perennial herb, up to 1.5m high, with a corm; occurring in grassland, especially along foothills and slopes of the southern Drakensberg Escarpment. Leaves arranged in a fan, narrowly sword-shaped, with the midrib and margins thickened and yellow, reaching at least to the base of the spike, with short hairs. Flowers usually 7–15, borne in an erect spike, ± two-ranked, large (mostly 80–110mm long), salmon to pale pink or mauve, lower three tepals with a reddish or purple stripe in the lower half.

A most attractive plant, cultivated in England as early as 1837. One of the principal species originally used to breed the large-flowered gladiolus hybrids, which are extensively grown as summer cut flowers and garden plants throughout the world today.

TOM DE WAAL

Watsonia borbonica (= *W. pyramidata*)

Iridaceae

E Pyramid watsonia **A** Pienksuurknol

Spring–Summer

Clump-forming perennial, up to 2m high, with a corm; occurring in fynbos, usually in well-drained sandy soils on rocky sandstone slopes. Leaves 20–40mm wide, glossy green. Flowers in an erect branched spike, the main axis with up to 20 flowers; perianth irregular; tepals spreading outward, with free part 26–36mm long, pale to deep pink to light purple, with a white streak at the base of each tepal; anthers violet.

A conspicuous species of the Cape Peninsula; flowers profusely after fire. Flowers are bee-pollinated. A popular garden plant; combines well with blue-flowered *Aristea major*. Plants die back and are dormant during summer. *W. rogersii*, with which it is often associated, has smaller flowers (tepals 22–25mm long) and narrower leaves (5–10mm wide).

COLIN PATERSON-JONES

Watsonia densiflora
E Natal watsonia **A** Natalse watsonia

Iridaceae
Summer

Erect, clump-forming perennial herb, up to 1.2m high, with a corm; occurring in grassland, especially along the coast. Leaves grey-green. Flowers ± 30–42, densely arranged in erect spikes; axis with densely packed, dry, brownish overlapping bracts; perianth bright pink with a darker pink line in the middle of each tepal.

A conspicuous and very floriferous species; often growing in extensive colonies. Requires plenty of water when grown in gardens. Plants are dormant during winter. Corms edible, also used in traditional medicine. *W. confusa* has pale blue-green leaves and spikes of 15–30 flowers; tends to occur more inland. *W. lepida*, centred in and around the Maluti and central Drakensberg mountains, usually grows as a solitary plant and is much smaller (up to 650mm high).

Watsonia strubeniae
E Graskop watsonia **A** Graskopse watsonia

Iridaceae
Summer

Erect perennial herb, up to 1m high, with a corm; occurring in grassland, often as scattered plants in large stands on mountain slopes. Leaves four or five in a fan, reaching to about the base of the spike. Flowers in long, slender, two- or three-branched, erect spikes; main spike has 25–35 flowers, side ones with fewer flowers; flowers pointing in opposite directions (two-ranked), irregular, funnel-shaped; tepals pale pink, each with a darker median stripe, free part 17–19mm long.

A most handsome plant that creates splashes of pink that contrast vividly with its green grassland habitat; threatened by commercial afforestation. Closely related to *W. transvaalensis* from the Graskop-Wolkberg area, that has larger flowers (tepals 20–25mm long) and a usually unbranched inflorescence.

Ballota africana (= *Marrubium africanum*)

Lamiaceae

E Cat herb **A** Kattekruid

Autumn–Spring

Soft, greyish, hairy perennial; occurring in fynbos and karroid vegetation, often along watercourses. Stems four-angled. Leaves opposite, rounded or ovate, densely covered with simple and star-shaped hairs; base cordate to rounded; margin irregularly toothed; venation conspicuously sunken above. Flowers in round clusters above each leaf pair; calyx funnel-shaped, persistent in fruit; corolla tubular, two-lipped, pink or purple.

Strongly scented when crushed. A very popular traditional medicine for a variety of ailments, including measles, colds, influenza, respiratory problems, heart trouble, piles and arthritis. Administered in the form of an infusion (a quarter cup fresh leaves and a few flower whorls, steeped in a cup of boiling water for about five minutes) or a brandy tincture.

Hemizygia transvaalensis

Lamiaceae

E Large hemizygia **A** Groot-hemizygia

Spring–Summer

Erect bushy shrublet, up to 1m high, with many annual stems from a woody perennial rootstock; occurring in grassland, often among rocks. Leaves opposite, sessile or with a very short stalk; blade usually ovate to broadly ovate, 15–40 × 8–22mm, dull green above and below. Flowers produced toward ends of shoots, in whorls of 3–6 flowers at each node; corolla tubular, two-lipped, 18–22mm long, whitish to mauve or lilac-pink; bracts very conspicuous, 12–24 × 4–10mm, bright pink.

Plants flower profusely after a fire; most of the colour being produced by the showy bracts rather than the flowers. Leaves and stems somewhat sticky and strongly aromatic when crushed. *H. thorncroftii*, mainly from the Barberton area, has flowers with a 14–16mm-long corolla.

Syncolostemon densiflorus

E Pink plume **A** Pienkpluim

Lamiaceae
Summer–Autumn

Sparingly branched perennial shrub, up to 2.5m high; occurring in grassland, usually along forest margins or in rocky places. Stems with short, white hairs. Leaves opposite; blade ovate or broadly elliptic to rounded, gland-dotted, with rough hairs. Flowers densely clustered in branched terminal inflorescences, in groups of 4–6 flowers; calyx reddish mauve; corolla two-lipped, 18–23mm long, pale to bright pink, rarely whitish; stamens protruding.

Most parts strongly aromatic when crushed; used in traditional medicine. Plants do not burn easily; forests may receive some protection against grassland fires from the dense stands often found along their margins – a type of natural firebreak. A very showy plant but difficult to maintain in gardens. *S. rotundifolius* (Pondoland) has flowers in clusters of two.

Hibiscus marlothianus

E Limestone hibiscus **A** Kalksteenhibiskus

Malvaceae
Summer–Autumn

Low-growing perennial herb, with a woody rootstock; occurring in grassland, bushveld and karroid vegetation, often on limestone or alkaline soils. Leaves deeply divided, often three-lobed, with unevenly toothed margins, sparingly covered with star-shaped hairs; stalk ± the same length as central lobe of leaf. Flowers pale to dark pink or whitish, with a dark purple centre; calyx of two dissimilar whorls, sepals of lower whorl ± half the length of those in the upper whorl.

Pollinated by honeybees. Flowers similar to those of *H. microcarpus* (red form), which has long, narrow, unlobed leaves. Also resembles the pink form of *H. aethiopicus*, which has oval leaves with a blunt tip. There are more than 50 species of *Hibiscus* in the region, most with yellow, pink or red flowers.

Hibiscus praeteritus

E Slender red hibiscus **A** Skraalrooihibiskus

Malvaceae

Summer

Erect, sparsely branched perennial shrublet, up to 2.5m high; occurring in bushveld, often along roadsides or river banks. Stems green, with coarse, star-shaped hairs. Leaves alternate, ovate, ± 20–30 × 10–20mm, sparsely dotted with star-shaped hairs; margin coarsely toothed; stalks slender, 5–10mm long. Flowers solitary, on long slender stalks in the axils of the upper leaves; lower calyx whorl with 10 narrow lobes; corolla 30mm in diameter, with five bright scarlet petals; staminal column twisted about 90° with five long style branches.

Although the flowers are relatively small, their brilliant coloration makes them very conspicuous. A number of rather similar looking scarlet-flowered *Hibiscus* species occur in the region. Expert knowledge is, however, required to distinguish between them.

Radyera urens

E Karoo pumpkin **A** Pampoenbossie

Malvaceae

Summer–Autumn

Perennial herb with robust, trailing stems; occurring in arid karroid vegetation types, often along roadsides. Leaves rounded, large (up to 120mm in diameter), grey-green and densely covered with star-shaped hairs, prominently veined below, erect on long stalks; base heart-shaped; margin crinkled. Flowers borne in leaf axils, often shaded by the leaves; petals deep red; stamens yellowish red, fused into a column around the style. Fruit a capsule opening with five valves.

A member of the hibiscus family, but with growth form and leaves superficially very similar to that of a pumpkin. An infusion of the root is used as a remedy against piles. Plants are not grazed by livestock. The genus, which has only this single species, is named after the eminent South African botanist, Robert Allen Dyer (1900–1987).

Dissotis canescens

E Pink marsh dissotis   **A** Pienkkalwerbossie

Melastomataceae
Summer

Perennial herb, up to 1.5m high, sprouting annually from an extensive underground rootstock; occurring in grassland and bushveld, usually in marshy situations and along streams. Stems four-angled, reddish brown. Leaves opposite, with 3–5 prominent veins from the base. Flowers in clusters near ends of stems, 35–45mm in diameter, bright pink.

Plants often grow in dense stands in marshes, resulting in mass displays of brilliant pink during flowering. Flowers are 'buzz pollinated'; when the anthers are vibrated by a bee, the fine powdery pollen is forcefully discharged through a tiny apical pore. Used medicinally to treat dysentery, diarrhoea and hangovers. Attractive plant for water features in gardens; requires soil rich in organic material, and full sun.

Nymania capensis

E Chinese lantern   **A** Klapperbos

Meliaceae
Winter–Spring

Rigid shrub or small tree, up to 3m high; occurring in hot semidesert areas, often along watercourses. Leaves ± linear, leathery, with dense hairs to hairless, unpleasantly scented when crushed. Flowers axillary, solitary, greenish pink to dark pink or scarlet, becoming bell-shaped with age. Fruit a papery, inflated capsule, creamy pink to bright reddish pink, with a silvery sheen.

Shoots and leaves very bitter due to limonoids (chemicals that deter herbivorous insects). Flowers have two strategies to ensure pollination. At first they are tubular with lots of nectar for attracting sunbirds, then they become bell-shaped and display the polliniferous stamens to attract honeybees. The fruit is wind-dispersed. Plants from the Little Karoo and Eastern Cape larger and less hairy than those from the Northern Cape.

Carpobrotus acinaciformis
E Pink sour fig **A** Pienksuurvy

Mesembryanthemaceae

Spring

Mat-forming perennial succulent, with robust trailing stems; occurring in fynbos and strandveld, usually on coastal dunes. Stems ± winged. Leaves opposite, three-angled, greyish green, often tinged with red. Flowers large (70–100mm in diameter), with short stalks and numerous rose-purple petals. Fruit fleshy, oval, yellowish brown, turning ± leathery when old.

Fresh leaves are chewed as a cure for sore throats; sap from the leaves is used as lotion for burns and blue-bottle stings. Fruit of this and other species used to make a delicious jam, but preparing it requires some skill. It is naturalised in parts of Italy. *C. edulis* has yellow flowers. Five other species occur in South Africa, often in sandy areas along the coast. Generic name derived from the Greek *karpos* = a fruit + *brotus* = edible.

Drosanthemum hispidum
E Common dew vygie **A** Gewone douvygie

Mesembryanthemaceae

Spring

Spreading, succulent perennial, up to 200mm high; occurring in karroid vegetation, often as extensive stands on flat sandy plains. Leaves opposite, cylindrical, covered by swollen water-storage cells that glisten in sunlight. Flowers up to 30mm in diameter, with numerous petals, bright pink.

Flowers open around midday and close by evening. As in most other members of the family, the dry seed capsules open in response to moisture. They have a complicated internal structure and function as splash cups; kinetic energy from raindrops is used to expel seed forcefully from the capsules. With almost 2,000 native species, Mesembryanthemaceae (mesembs or vygies) is by far the most important family of succulents in the region. Most species are found in the Succulent Karoo Biome.

Commicarpus pentandrus
E Cerise stars **A** Veldpatat

Nyctaginaceae
Summer

Perennial herb with annual trailing stems, sprouting from a large tuberous rootstock; occurring in grassland, bushveld and karroid vegetation, often along roadsides. Leaves opposite, widely spaced, ovate, ± 40mm in diameter. Flowers in whorls at tips of slender, erect stalks, borne all along the trailing stems; corolla funnel-shaped, bright pink. Fruit with ± five large, sticky, purplish-brown glands.

An unmistakable species that often forms large, brilliantly coloured patches flat on the ground. Plants grow very old and some of the larger underground tubers may be more than a century old. Tubers edible; they are either cooked or baked under hot ash. Grazed by livestock. Seeds dispersed by animals; glandular fruit adheres to clothing and animal hides.

Cycnium racemosum
E Large pink ink plant **A** Berginkplant

Orobanchaceae
Summer–Autumn

Erect, usually unbranched, perennial herb, up to 800mm high; occurring in grassland, usually in rocky places. Stems ± four-angled, often tinged with purple. Leaves opposite below, alternate higher up the stem, ± 80 × 20mm, rough; margin toothed, purplish red. Flowers in terminal racemes, alternate or in pairs; corolla large, ± 60mm in diameter, usually deep pink with a whitish centre, sweetly scented.

A very conspicuous and most attractive hemiparasite. Known host plants include various grasses and species of *Acalypha*. Bruised flowers turn black, hence the common names. Used medicinally as an emetic and as a general painkiller. Generic name derived from the Latin *cygnus* (= a swan) in reference to the white flowers of *C. adonense*, a low-growing grassland species.

Graderia scabra

E Wild penstemon A Wilde penstemon

Orobanchaceae

Spring

Tufted herb with annual shoots from a perennial rootstock, up to 600mm high; occurring in grassland. Leaves alternate, stalkless, overlapping, ± 50 × 15mm, roughly hairy; margin smooth, with a few coarse teeth. Flowers in leafy terminal racemes; corolla irregular, pink, rarely white, outer surface with short hairs; filaments hairy toward base only. Fruit a capsule, many-seeded.

Flowers profusely after late winter or early spring fires. Used in traditional medicine for various ailments. *G. subintegra* is very common in Highveld grassland; it has leaves that are not rough to the touch and filaments with hairs along almost their entire length. The name *Graderia* is an anagram of *Gerardia*, the name of a genus confined to the New World and presently known as *Agalinis*.

Striga elegans

E Large witchweed A Grootrooiblom

Orobanchaceae

Summer–Autumn

Slender, erect herb; stem simple or, rarely, slightly branched; occurring in grassland. Leaves opposite, stiff, erect, covered with minute, rough hairs. Flowers borne toward tips of stems; corolla irregular, 12–20mm long, two-lipped, upper lip not much shorter than the lower lip, scarlet on inner and orange-yellow on outer surface. Fruit a capsule, many-seeded.

A root parasite of grasses, although rarely attacking crop plants. It is classified as a hemiparasite, because the plant contains chlorophyll and is therefore partly self-sustaining. *S. asiatica* has smaller flowers (12mm long) with the upper lip of the corolla much shorter than the lower. It is often found as a parasite on maize, sorghum and sugar cane. Cultural methods of control are employed to eradicate plants from crops.

Oxalis purpurea
E Pink sorrel **A** Pienksuring

Oxalidaceae
Autumn–Spring

Low-growing perennial herb, up to 150mm high, with tuberous bulbs; occurring in fynbos and disturbed places, often in large colonies. Leaves in a basal rosette, palmately compound, with three rounded leaflets. Flowers solitary, erect, on slender stalks; corolla with lobes spirally twisted, bright pink with a yellow centre.

A native plant that often occurs as a weed on lawns in the southwestern Cape. Flowers open in response to bright sunlight. The leaves have an acidic taste and are used as a vegetable, to flavour food, or as a replacement for salt. Tubers are peeled, cooked and served like potatoes. The region is a major centre of diversity for *Oxalis*, with more than 130 species in the Cape Floristic Kingdom alone. Many native members have considerable horticultural potential.

Ceratotheca triloba
E Wild foxglove **A** Vingerhoedblom

Pedaliaceae
Summer

Erect annual herb, up to 2m high, most parts covered with fine hairs; occurring mainly in bushveld, usually along roadsides and in disturbed places. Leaves opposite, ± deeply divided into three lobes; margin bluntly toothed. Flowers borne on short stalks in axils of leaves along upper portion of stems, drooping; corolla pale pink to mauve, lower lip with purplish stripes, and fine hairs. Fruit a hairy capsule with two horns at the tip.

Unpleasantly scented when crushed. A tea made from the leaves is used in traditional medicine, especially for intestinal disorders. Together with other ingredients, it makes an effective insect-repellent spray, especially for aphids on roses and pot plants. Its use on vegetables is not recommended, because of its fetid odour.

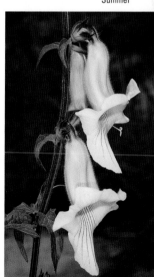

Dicerocaryum senecioides

E Devil's thorn **A** Elandsdoring

Pedaliaceae
Summer–Autumn

Mat-forming perennial herb, with long, trailing, annual stems from a woody rootstock; occurring in bushveld, often along roadsides or in sandy places. Leaves grey-green above, powdery white below; margin deeply lobed. Flowers borne all along the stem, on slender, erect stalks; corolla irregular, pink, with darker nectar guides. Fruit a flattened, elliptic and very hard disc lying flat on the ground, with two very sharp, erect spikes on the upper surface.

Fresh plant material crushed in water yields a mucilaginous mass formerly used as soap substitute. Leaves rubbed with water between the hands yield a soapy lather; formerly also used in rural areas as a lubricant for childbirth. The spiny fruit is able to penetrate hoofs and feet causing considerable pain.

Pterodiscus speciosus

E Water potato **A** Ruiterblom

Pedaliaceae
Summer

Semisucculent perennial herb, sprouting annually from a thick, fleshy tuber; occurring in grassland and bushveld. Leaves linear-lanceolate, greyish green; ± fleshy; margin toothed. Flowers ± solitary in leaf axils, with short stalks; corolla broadly funnel-shaped, weakly irregular, dark pink, outside of floral tube with minute whitish dots. Fruit with four longitudinal wings.

Tubers edible when fresh. Also used to brew a beer; tubers are peeled, dried, pounded, mixed with cold water and honey and allowed to ferment. Two dark purple-black glands (extrafloral nectaries) are located at the base of each flower stalk. These structures secrete a sweet substance and are eagerly visited by ants. Apparently the presence of ants deters other herbivorous insects that may damage the plant.

Sesamum triphyllum
E Wild sesame **A** Wildesesam

Pedaliaceae
Spring–Summer

An erect, sparsely branched annual or short-lived perennial herb, up to 1.5m high; occurring in grassland and bushveld, often along roadsides and in disturbed places. Leaves opposite, simple to deeply palmately divided, unpleasantly scented; margin sometimes faintly toothed. Flowers solitary, axillary, with short stalks; corolla brownish pink, dark pink to bluish pink. Fruit a cylindrical capsule with a pointed tip, splitting in half when ripe (hence expression 'open sesame').

Flower stalks each subtended by small black glands (extrafloral nectaries); these attract ants, the presence of which deters insect herbivores. Seeds edible and rich in oil. Sesame seed, from *S. orientale*, is the oldest grown oil seed (since ± 3,500–3,050 BC). *S. alatum* usually has brighter pink flowers and simple leaves.

Saltera sarcocolla
E Fly bush **A** Vlieëbos

Penaeaceae
All year

Sparsely branched, rather untidy perennial shrublet, up to 1m high; occurring in fynbos, usually in sandy soils derived from sandstone. Leaves opposite, rounded, leathery, overlapping, four-ranked. Flowers clustered at ends of stems, surrounded by sticky, bract-like leaves; corolla usually pink, often with white markings, sticky.

Small insects get stuck in the sticky secretions of the bracts and flowers, hence the common names. Penaeaceae is one of eight plant families that are endemic or near-endemic to the Cape Floristic Kingdom. *Sonderothamnus speciosus* (mainly Klein River Mountains near Hermanus) has leaves with a thickened, dark-coloured tip; they are very neatly arranged, mainly along the upper parts of the stems. Flowers surrounded by fringed bracts, neither being sticky.

Melinis repens (= *Rhynchelytrum repens*)

E Natal red top **A** Natalse rooipluim

Poaceae
Summer–Autumn

Annual or short-lived perennial grass, up to 0.8m high, growing in tufts; occurring mainly in grassland, bushveld and karroid vegetation, often in disturbed places, especially abundant along roadsides and in fallow fields. Leaves bright green, with expanded blades and a prominent midrib. Inflorescence a much-branched panicle; spikelets hairy, various shades of pink, fading to white.

One of the most common and widespread grasses in the region. A beautiful sight when growing in dense stands on the shoulders of roads. Palatable pioneer or sub-climax grass; plays an important role in stabilising disturbed soil. Used in flower arrangements. *M. nerviglumis*, a perennial with more compact silvery-pink inflorescences, grows on rocky hillsides; it has thread-like (rolled), blue-green leaves.

BRAAM VAN WYK & SASA MALAN

Nylandtia spinosa (= *Muraltia spinosa*)

E Tortoise berry **A** Skilpadbessie

Polygalaceae
Autumn–Spring

Much-branched, rigid shrub, up to 4m high; young twigs spine-tipped; occurring in fynbos, renosterveld and strandveld; usually in sandy soils. Branches short, robust; side branches usually transformed into short spines. Leaves very small, thick. Flowers produced along branches, irregular, purple, pink or white; petals three, united at the base, lower one keel-like, enclosing the stamens, with a lobed appendage below its tip. Fruit a globose berry, shiny and red when ripe.

Berries edible, but with an astringent taste; eaten by birds, tortoises and people. Fruit, leaves and young twigs used medicinally for the treatment of tuberculosis and stomach disorders. *N. scoparia* (= *Muraltia scoparia*) has elongated, slender branches, side branches not transformed into short spines, and leaves that are usually absent at flowering.

Polygala virgata
E Purple broom   **A** Bloukappies

Polygalaceae
All year

Slender, single-stemmed shrub, up to 3m tall, sparsely branched in the upper third; occurring in grassland and along forest margins. Leaves narrowly elliptic, ± 20–90 × 1–20mm, with short stalks, often dropping before flowering. Flowers in long, terminal racemes, pink to purplish pink; wings (enlarged sepals) with dark purplish veins; keel with a brush-like appendage.

Widely cultivated in gardens for its attractive flowers and extended flowering period. Flowers superficially similar to those of members of the pea family (Fabaceae). Known as 'keel flowers', they are functionally adapted for bee pollination. In its search for nectar, the visiting bee depresses the movable keel petal, whereupon the sexual organs are released and touch the insect, either depositing or picking up pollen, thus effecting pollination.

Mimetes cucullatus
E Common pagoda   **A** Rooistompie

Proteaceae
All year

Shrub, up to 2m high, with many erect stems from a large rootstock; occurring in fynbos. Leaves oblong-elliptic, hairless; apex with 1–3 teeth, each tipped by a reddish gland. Flowers in large, cylindrical inflorescences at the ends of stems, topped by a crown of flat, reduced red leaves; flowers subtended and clasped from above by orange-red leaves; tepals white, hairy.

The showy part of the inflorescence is provided by the colourful leaves interspersed between the flowers. Seed with a fleshy appendage; collected and taken underground by ants. Plants rapidly resprout after fire. This is the most widespread of the 13 species of *Mimetes*, a genus endemic to the Cape Floristic Kingdom. Most of the species have a very local distribution and at least one is already considered extinct.

Agathosma ovata

Rutaceae

🇪 Oval-leaved buchu 🇦 Basterboegoe

All year

Bushy shrublet, up to 500mm high, sprouting from a perennial rootstock; occurring in grassland and fynbos. Leaves oval to roundish, ± 15mm long, dull green above, shiny bright green below; margin recurved. Flowers borne among leaves toward ends of branches, ± 10mm in diameter; petals five, free, pink to white.

A wide-ranging and very variable species. A member of the citrus family, most parts have a strong citrus scent when crushed. Used medicinally to treat nervous disorders and other ailments. About 140 species of *Agathosma* occur in the region, most of them confined to the Cape Floristic Kingdom. Leaves of *A. betulina* and *A. crenulata* are the main sources of the buchu of commerce, a popular traditional remedy against kidney and urinary-tract infections.

Diascia namaquensis

Scrophulariaceae

🇪 Namaqualand twinspur 🇦 Namakwalandse horinkie

Winter–Spring

Erect annual herb, up to 400mm high; occurring in karroid vegetation and fynbos, usually in sandy places. Leaves opposite; margin toothed. Flowers solitary at the ends of erect stalks, irregular, pink to purple-red, with two prominent spurs or sacs on the lower back surface of the corolla.

The spurs contain glandular hairs on the inside near the tips. These hairs secrete oil, which is collected by solitary bees of the genus *Rediviva*. As a bee alights on the flower, it inserts its long forelegs into the two spurs. Once inside the spurs, special hairs on the bee's legs absorb the oil. In the process pollen is transferred from the flower to the visiting bee; the bee then effects pollination when it visits the next flower. Forelegs of the bees often closely match the length of the spurs of their host plant.

Phygelius aequalis
E River bells **A** Rivierklokkie

Scrophulariaceae
Summer–Autumn

Herbaceous perennial shrublet, up to 1m high; occurring along stream banks in montane grassland. Stems four-angled. Leaves opposite, oval, 75–100 × 40mm, dark green above, pale green below, soft-textured; margin toothed; stalk ± 25mm long. Flowers in a rather compact terminal panicle, drooping; corolla ± 40mm long, pale pinkish red, lobes ± subequal, outlined in deep red, yellow on the inside; stamens and style exserted. Fruit a capsule.

Flowers are pollinated by sunbirds. Used in traditional medicine. A cold-hardy plant suitable for moist sites in temperate gardens. *P. capensis* is the only other species in the genus. It has drooping, coral-red flowers in lax panicles; these are borne on stalks that are sharply bent so that the flowers point toward the main inflorescence axis.

**Lantana camara*
E Lantana **A** Lantana

Verbenaceae
Summer–Winter

Much-branched perennial shrub; invading grassland, bushveld and forest margins, often occurring in disturbed places under and among trees. Stems four-angled, with scattered, recurved prickles. Leaves opposite, with rough hairs, unpleasantly scented when crushed. Flowers congested in flat-topped heads, predominant colour very variable, including pink, yellow, orange or orange-brown. Fruit fleshy, globose, shiny black.

A native of Central and South America; cultivated for ornament and hedging. Poisonous to livestock. This is a declared weed in South Africa. Flowers open successively toward the centre of the inflorescence and usually change colour as they fade. This colour change probably signals to pollinating insects which flowers have been pollinated, and which have not.

118

Barleria obtusa
🇪 Bush violet 🇦 Bosviooltjie

Acanthaceae
Autumn

Sprawling perennial shrublet, which is rather untidy in appearance; occurring in grassland, thicket and bushveld, often in semishade and associated with rocky outcrops or clusters of trees and shrubs. Most parts with soft, silky hairs. Leaves opposite, oval, ± 50 × 30mm, dark green, with very short stalks. Flowers in clusters of 1–4, mainly toward ends of branchlets, slightly irregular; petals usually blue, rarely white or pink, with the throat darker than the lobes; anthers deep blue. Fruit a flattened capsule, with 1–4 seeds.

A very floriferous species widely grown in gardens; easily cultivated from cuttings. Flowers attract butterflies that probably act as pollinators. Dry capsules dehisce explosively when moistened to release the flattened seeds. Browsed by livestock and game.

Agapanthus inapertus
🇪 Drooping agapanthus 🇦 Drakensbergbloulelie

Agapanthaceae
Summer

Deciduous perennial herb, up to 1.5m high, with a rhizome and numerous fleshy roots; occurring in high-rainfall grassland or scrub, often associated with rocky outcrops, forest margins or stream banks. Leaves bluish green, basally overlapping and forming a stem-like structure. Flowers in umbels, deep blue to almost purple-black; tepals tubular, not (or only slightly) spreading; stalks erect in bud, becoming drooping or pendulous in open flowers.

An aggregate species with many different forms. Floral colour may vary from blue to purple-black in the same population. An attractive garden plant, but less frequently grown than the next species. The generic name is derived from the Greek *agape* = love and *anthos* = flower; *inapertus* means 'closed', alluding to the tubular flowers.

Agapanthus praecox
E Common agapanthus **A** Gewone bloulelie

Agapanthaceae
Summer

Evergreen perennial herb, up to 1.5m high, with a rhizome and numerous fleshy roots; occurring in high-rainfall grassland, often along forest margins or in rocky places. Leaves dark green, not aggregated into a stem-like structure at the base. Flowers in umbels, pale blue or rarely white, with a short tube and spreading tepals; stalks erect or spreading. Fruit a capsule; seed numerous, flat, winged, shiny black.

A very popular garden plant throughout the world. In traditional medicine a decoction of the rhizome and roots, or water in which a plant was grown, are widely used by women before and after childbirth. Crude extracts of the plant have a proven effect on the contraction of the uterus wall. *Agapanthus* is a genus of about 10 species, all confined to southern Africa.

Berkheya purpurea
E Purple berkheya **A** Persdisseldoring

Asteraceae
Summer–Autumn

Stout, very spiny perennial herb, up to 1m high, with a single, central stem; occurring in damp, high-altitude montane grassland, often in large colonies. Stem with spiny longitudinal wings. Leaves mainly in a basal rosette, dark green with rough hairs above and white felt below; margin coarsely toothed, with sharp spines. Flower heads (see page 142) with ray florets pale to deep mauve, rarely white, disc florets purple.

Berkheya is named after the Dutch botanist, Jan le Francq van Berkhey (1729–1812). Most of the ± 75 species are confined to South Africa. Flower heads in the genus are commonly yellow, *B. purpurea* being the only member with purple flowers. These very beautiful plants are virtually impossible to handle because of all the spines.

*Cichorium intybus

E Chicory **A** Sigorei

Asteraceae
Spring–Summer

Erect perennial herb, up to 1m high, with a fleshy taproot; occurring near areas of human habitation, especially in moist places. Basal leaves large, with the margin irregularly toothed and lobed. Flower heads (see page 142) comprising only strap-like ray florets, clear pale blue, borne in clusters of two or three on well-branched, ± leafless stems.

A native of Asia and Europe. Introduced as an agricultural crop and now naturalised in many parts of the region. Flowers open in the morning and close by midday. The leaves are cooked as a spinach, but at least two changes of water are required to remove bitter principles. Root used as a diluent of coffee, a coffee substitute, an adulterant and to extract locust antifeedants (chemicals that deter locusts). Leaf, stem and root are also widely used in traditional medicine.

Felicia filifolia

E Fine-leaved felicia **A** Persbergdraaibos

Asteraceae
Spring

Erect, much-branched, ± evergreen perennial shrublet, up to 1m high; occurring in grassland and karroid shrubland. Stems pale creamy brown. Leaves in tufts, needle-like. Flower heads (see page 142) borne in profusion along the length of the stem, aromatic; ray florets mauve to white; disc florets yellow.

Four subspecies are recognised. Subspecies *filifolia* is the most widespread and often proliferates in overgrazed grassland. Although not very palatable to livestock (apparently poisonous in some areas), it imparts a characteristic flavour to meat. Plants are very attractive when in flower and are occasionally grown in gardens. Subspecies *schaeferi* (*kleingombos*), a smaller plant, is much more palatable to livestock; it is mainly confined to the winter-rainfall Karoo region (Succulent Karoo Biome).

Hilliardiella aristata (= *Vernonia natalensis*)

Asteraceae

Spring

E Silver bitterbush **A** Silverbitterbossie

Silvery, erect, many-stemmed perennial herb, up to 1m high, with a woody rootstock; occurring in grassland. Leaves with short stalk (up to 2mm) or stalkless, long and narrow, 35–60 × 4–15mm; base tapering; both surfaces with silvery silky hairs. Flower heads (see page 142) in a cluster at end of each stem, comprising disc florets only, purple; bracts surrounding head with long, curved tips.

Plants often occur in large colonies; easily recognised from a distance by their silvery colour. Various parts of the plant are used in traditional medicine to treat coughs, malaria and many other ailments. Leaves and roots are used by the Zulu as charms against lightning. May be confused with *H. oligocephala* (see next entry), a species with the leaves rounded at the base and ± hairless above.

Hilliardiella oligocephala (= *Vernonia oligocephala*)

Asteraceae

Spring

E Bicoloured-leaved bitterbush **A** Bitterbossie

Robust or slender, erect perennial shrublet, up to 1m high, with few to many stems sprouting from a woody rootstock; occurring in grassland. Leaves almost stalkless, oval to ovate; base rounded; apex often ending abruptly in a sharp point; dull green and ± hairless above, densely covered with silvery hairs below. Flower heads (see page 142) about 10mm in diameter, numerous, clustered together in ± flat-topped groups at ends of shoots, dark purple.

A tea prepared from the leaves is a popular and tried remedy against mild forms of diabetes. Also used as a disinfectant and to treat many other ailments. The tea is extremely bitter (hence the Afrikaans name) – a taste probably imparted by the presence of sesquiterpenoid lactones, compounds with antibacterial and antifungal properties.

Vernonia fastigiata

E Narrow-leaved vernonia **A** Smalblaarbitterbossie

Asteraceae

Spring–Summer

Annual or short-lived perennial herb, which is usually much-branched and twiggy; occurring mainly in bushveld and associated grassland, often a weed in disturbed places, particularly along roadsides. Leaves sparsely present, stalkless, ± 40 × 4mm; margin smooth. Flower heads (see page 142) produced at tips of stems, ± 20mm in diameter, purple, consisting of disc florets only; bracts long, bristle-tipped, recurved and woolly.

Plants are extended bloomers and flower heads are produced virtually throughout the growing season. The flower heads are extremely popular among a great variety of butterflies, and the presence of the plants can be recognised at a distance from the mere aggregation of these insects. In *V. poskeana* (= *Polydora poskeana*) the involucral bracts are usually neither spreading nor recurved.

**Echium plantagineum*

E Purple bugloss **A** Pers-echium

Boraginaceae

Spring

Annual or biennial herb, with one to many flowering stems, up to 0.8m high; most parts with soft, appressed hairs; occurring along roadsides, in waste ground and as a weed of cultivation. Basal leaves ovate to oblanceolate; side veins prominent above and below. Upper stem leaves stalkless; base heart-shaped. Flowers broadly funnel-shaped, blue or deep purplish blue; stamens five, of which two protrude.

A native of western Europe, southwestern Britain and the Mediterranean region. Rather similar to *E. vulgare*, a native of Europe, which is also naturalised in the region. The latter occurs mainly along the southern and central Drakensberg. Its basal leaves are narrowly lanceolate, the side veins are not prominent, and the stem leaves have tapering bases; flowers with four stamens protruding.

Lobostemon fruticosus

E Eight-day healing bush **A** Agtdaegeneesbos

Boraginaceae
Spring

 Soft-wooded, silvery, laxly branched perennial shrub, up to 2.5m high; occurring in fynbos, locally abundant in sandy places on flats and mountain slopes. Leaves strap-shaped, 15–60 × 5–12mm, with dense hairs, aromatic when crushed; margin smooth. Flowers in clusters near ends of branches; corolla funnel-shaped, in various subtle shades of blue and pink, even in the same plant, rarely white, with short hairs.

Early colonists at the Cape used an infusion of the leaves to treat body sores and other skin eruptions such as ringworm. The salve was thought to bring about healing within eight days, hence the common names. Distantly related to comfrey and borage, two popular Eurasian medicinal plants of the same family, with similar wound-healing properties.

Heliophila coronopifolia

E Blue sporrie **A** Blou-sporrie

Brassicaceae
Spring

 Erect annual herb, up to 0.6m high, often freely branched above; occurring in fynbos and renosterveld. Leaves simple or pinnately lobed, with a greyish bloom; lobes up to 3mm wide. Flowers bright blue with a white or pale greenish-yellow centre. Fruit 30–90 × 1.3–2mm, constricted at regular intervals between the seed, giving a beaded appearance.

There are ± 70 species of *Heliophila* in the region, most with vivid blue flowers, the rest white- and yellow-flowered (common among spring flowers in Namaqualand). Flowers tend mainly to open on warm, sunny days, hence the name *Heliophila*, which means 'sun-lover'. Although the individual flowers are extremely dainty, plants often grow in dense masses, resulting in spectacular shows of colour.

Commelina livingstonii

Commelinaceae

E Livingston's blue commelina **A** Gewone blouselblom

Summer

Perennial herb with spreading, branched stems from a woody crown, usually hairy; occurring in grassland and bushveld. Leaves narrowly ovate, ± 70 × 20mm, folded along midrib, greyish green. Flowering spathes clustered at tips of stems, ± stalkless, folded with margins joined at the base, outer surface finely ribbed, with bristly hairs; flowers opening one at a time, pale to dark blue.

The boat-shaped spathes are filled with a clear, tasteless and somewhat viscous liquid that covers the young, developing flower buds. When a bud is ready to open, it pulls from the liquid, emerges from the spathe and unfolds its very delicate petals in early morning, only to fade by noon. There are about 10 species of *Commelina* with blue or mauve flowers in the region.

Cyanotis speciosa (= *C. nodiflora*)

Commelinaceae

E Doll's powderpuff **A** Bloupoeierkwassie

Spring–Summer

Perennial herb that sprouts annually from a short rhizome, up to 400mm high; occurring in grassland. Leaves clustered in a basal rosette, ± channelled, lower surface with short, ± erect hairs. Flowers on erect inflorescences, in clusters of 1–3, blue, purple, mauve or pink; stamens very hairy, creating the impression of a powder puff and providing most of the colour, anthers white.

Flowers open in the morning and fade by midday. Floral colour varies across its range, usually more bluish toward the west and more pinkish toward the east. Roots used for medicinal and magical purposes. *Cyanotis lapidosa* has leaves with appressed hairs on both surfaces and ± reclining inflorescences. It grows in colonies in rocky areas.

Streptocarpus primulifolius
E Primula-leaved streptocarpus **A** Primulablaar-streptocarpus

Gesneriaceae
Summer–Autumn

Perennial herb with a stout,
horizontal rhizome; occurring
in the understorey of forest,
often on rock faces. Leaves in
a basal rosette, up to 450 × 110mm, hairy.
Inflorescence erect, up to 260mm high, with
1–4 flowers; corolla large, 65–90mm long,
pale bluish violet with broad, reddish-purple
nectar guides.

Closely related to *S. formosus*, which
has a yellow corolla-tube floor with purple-
brown lines (coastal forests of Transkei and
southern KwaZulu-Natal). About 50 species
of *Streptocarpus* occur in the region, most
associated with forest. *S. wendlandii* is
one of several rarities in the group. It has
a single large leaf up to 500 × 400mm,
the latter being dark green above and
deep purplish red below; plants die after
flowering. It is confined to the Ngoye Forest
in KwaZulu-Natal.

Merwilla plumbea (= *Scilla natalensis*)
E Large blue scilla **A** Blouslangkop

Hyacinthaceae
Spring–Summer

Deciduous perennial herb, up
to 1m high, sprouting annually
from a large bulb located
half-above ground; occurring
singly or in colonies in moist grassland, often
in rocky places. Leaves erect, up to 500mm
long, grey-green. Flowers distinctly stalked,
borne in a raceme on a sturdy stalk up to 1m
high, usually produced with the new leaves,
pale to deep purplish blue.

A variable species, but readily identified
by its robust habit; some of the smaller
plants formerly classified under this name are
now treated as separate species. The bulb
is extensively used in traditional medicine
to treat various ailments, including sprains,
boils, sores, female infertility and internal
tumours. An attractive, frost-resistant garden
plant; for best results bulbs should be planted
partly above ground and left undisturbed for
many years.

Aristea major (= A. thyrsiflora)

E Giant aristea **A** Blousuurknol

Iridaceae

Spring

A robust evergreen perennial, up to 1.5m high, sprouting from a rhizome and forming dense clumps; occurring in fynbos, usually in marshy places on mountain slopes. Leaves erect, rigid, long and strap-shaped, bluish green, leathery. Flowers borne in dense clusters on long inflorescences, regular, bright blue, with a satiny lustre. Fruit a capsule.

An attractive species, even when not in flower; widely cultivated in gardens, even thriving in semishade. Attractively combined with yellow *Wachendorfia thyrsiflora* (page 47) and pink *Watsonia borbonica* (page 102). Plants should be kept moist throughout the year. Individual flowers are short-lived, they open in the morning and shrivel up after midday, the tepals twisting as they fade. Fortunately, new buds open continuously over a long period.

GERALD CUBITT

Moraea polystachya

E Karoo blue tulp **A** Karoobloutulp

Iridaceae

Autumn–Winter

Erect perennial, up to 0.8m high, with a corm; occurring in arid karroid shrubland, on stony/shale flats or on rocky slopes, often proliferating in overgrazed areas. Leaves 3–5, long and narrow, channelled to almost flat. Flowers violet to pale blue; tepals six, outer three with yellow to orange nectar guides.

Plants often occur in dense stands, imparting a blue colour to the veld when in flower. Although the individual flowers last only a single day, the flowering period may continue for up to six weeks. Extremely poisonous to cattle and sheep, with death occurring 24–48 hours after ingestion of the plants. Newly introduced or hungry livestock are most at risk. Animals raised on tulp-infested veld learn to avoid it. The toxic principles are cardioactive glycosides (bufadienolides).

Moraea tripetala

E Dainty moraea **A** Blou-uintjie

Iridaceae
Spring

Slender, erect perennial, up to 0.5m high, with a corm; occurring in arid karroid shrubland, fynbos and renosterveld, both on clay and sandy soils. Leaves solitary or rarely two, long and narrow. Flowers usually pale to dark blue to purple, with only the outer three of the six tepals well developed.

An easily recognised species on account of the apparently absent but actually very reduced inner tepals. Among the major colour variants are plants with attractive yellow or sometimes pinkish flowers. It is probably pollinated by small carpenter bees. Of the ± 120 species of *Moraea*, no less than 65 are restricted to the winter-rainfall area of South Africa. All are characterised by iris-like flowers, which are usually short-lived, lasting less than a day; some may open in the late afternoon and fade shortly after sunset.

Plectranthus ecklonii

E Large spur-flower bush **A** Persmuishondblaar

Lamiaceae
Summer–Autumn

A perennial, soft-wooded and much-branched shrub, up to 2.5m high; occurring in the understorey of forest. Leaves 60–170 × 40–100mm, with very few hairs; venation prominently raised below; margin toothed. Flowers borne in profusion in branched terminal panicles; corolla purplish blue, narrow, up to 20mm long, gradually expanding to the throat, not expanded at the base.

An attractive plant for shady gardens; pink and white cultivars are popular. The leaves, which have an unpleasant odour when crushed, are used traditionally to treat headaches and hayfever. About 45 species of *Plectranthus* occur in the region, most of them confined to the high-rainfall eastern and northern parts. The group is well known for its aromatic leaves, attractive flowers and preference for shady habitats.

Pycnostachys urticifolia

E Large hedgehog bush **A** Groot-ystervarksalie

Lamiaceae
Autumn–Winter

Sparsely branched, soft-wooded perennial shrub, up to 3m high; occurring in grassland and bushveld, usually in marshy places, along stream banks or forest margins. Leaves broadly ovate, distinctly stalked; margin toothed. Flowers in spikes at tips of branches, dark blue or rarely white; corolla with lower lip large and boat-shaped; calyx persistent in fruit, the pointed lobes developing into sharp, reddish spines.

Flowers open in succession, with rarely more than three rows open at a time. Occasionally planted in gardens, but plants are frost-sensitive and not very showy. The common names refer to the spiny inflorescences. *P. reticulata* has essentially stalkless, linear to lanceolate leaves; it is more widespread in the region. Generic name from the Greek *pyknos* = dense + *stachys* = a spike.

Salvia africana-caerulea (= *S. africana*)

E Cape blue sage **A** Kaapse blousalie

Lamiaceae
Spring–Summer

Sparingly branched perennial shrub, up to 2m high; occurring in coastal fynbos and on rocky slopes. Leaves greyish green, obovate-elliptic to broadly obovate, hairy. Flowers in whorls of 2–6 among persistent bracts, 5–12 of these whorls arranged in spike-like inflorescences; corolla pale blue to bluish purple or pinkish, lower lip with a paler blue margin and white to yellowish in the centre.

Most parts strongly aromatic when crushed. One of the first plants used by the Dutch at the Cape as a household medicine. A bitter-tasting tea prepared from the leaves is popular as a treatment for colds, flu and various other ailments; sugar, honey or lemon juice may be added. Plants are easily propagated by cuttings. *S. chamelaeagnea* has two-flowered whorls arranged in large panicles, and deciduous bracts.

JOHN MANNING

Tetradenia riparia (= *Iboza riparia*)

E Gingerbush **A** Gemmerbos

Lamiaceae
Winter

Robust, deciduous, somewhat succulent, perennial shrub, up to about 3m high; occurring in bushveld, usually on rocky hillsides and along streams in relatively frost-free areas. Stems stout, brittle, four-angled when young. Leaves velvety; margin toothed. Inflorescences large, spreading, diffusely branched, the ultimate branchlets spike-like; flowers very small, mauve or rarely white.

Most parts are strongly lavender scented when crushed. Flowering takes place when plants are leafless in winter, creating the impression of a mauve mist. Plants are either male (illustrated) or female, with the female spikes being more compact. An attractive garden plant for frost-free areas; easily grown from cuttings. Widely used in traditional medicine. *Iboza* is a Zulu vernacular name for the species.

Lobelia coronopifolia

E Coastal lobelia **A** Kus-lobelia

Lobeliaceae
All year

Perennial herb, up to 0.6m high, sprouting from a woody rootstock; occurring in coastal grassland, usually in sandy soil. Leaves in a basal rosette, 20–45 × 1–3mm; margin toothed. Flowers sparsely arranged in terminal racemes; corolla ± 25mm long, purplish blue, irregular, with three large lower lobes and two small, recurved upper lobes, the latter resembling horns.

All parts of the plant contain a milky latex. Flowers are visited by honeybees and butterflies. The leaf is used in traditional medicine; some members of the genus contain lobeline, an alkaloid with similar but less potent properties than nicotine. Propagated from seed or cuttings, it makes an attractive and hardy garden plant. The genus is named after Matthias de l'Obel (1538–1616), a famous Flemish nobleman, physician and botanist.

Lobelia erinus (= *L. nuda*)

E Wild lobelia **A** Wilde-lobelia

Lobeliaceae

Spring

Small, slender, erect annual herb; occurring in grassland and fallow fields, usually in moist places. Leaves concentrated toward base, sometimes ± in a basal rosette; blade usually 4–20mm wide, narrowing into a stalk-like base or with stalks up to 15mm long. Flowers borne on slender stalks in a branched inflorescence, pale blue; base of lower lip with a large, white blotch; throat yellow.

Plants often form extensive stands in seasonally wet places in grassland. When these stands flower simultaneously in early spring, the resultant large patches of blue create an extremely realistic illusion of pools of water. Powdered roots and leaves are mixed with a little water and sniffed to clear a blocked nose. About 80 species of *Lobelia* are native to the region.

Dissotis princeps

E Purple dissotis **A** Perskalwerbos

Melastomataceae

Summer–Winter

Robust perennial herb or a much-branched shrub, up to 3m high, most parts with short, bristly hairs; occurring in grassland and bushveld, usually in swampy places or along streams. Leaves opposite, usually lanceolate to ovate-lanceolate; lamina with 5–7 prominent veins from the base. Flowers in sparse or compact terminal clusters; petals ± 25 × 20mm, lilac to dark purple or violet, rarely white; anthers unequal, purple.

Each anther has a tiny pore at the tip. For the dry, powdery pollen to be released, the anthers need to be vibrated ('buzzed') by a bee at a specific frequency. The vibration causes the pollen grains to resonate inside the anther, resulting in their forceful release from the pore. The root is used in traditional medicine; formerly also as a famine food.

Nymphaea nouchali (= *N. caerulea*; *N. capensis*)
E Blue waterlily **A** Blouwaterlelie

Nymphaeaceae
All year

Aquatic herb with floating leaves and a tuberous rhizome; occurring in standing freshwater pools, pans and dams, or in slow-moving streams. Flowers pale blue to mauve, with a centre of yellow stamens compactly arranged around the stigma to form a fluid-filled stigmatic cup, 25–35mm in diameter, which functions like a pit trap.

When an insect lands on a stamen, the filament bends inward causing the insect to fall into the cup, where it is retained through various mechanisms. Insects are digested in the older, submerged flowers (a primitive insectivory). Tubers are boiled or roasted by rural people as a vegetable, but are spongy and rather tasteless. Seed, pounded to meal, may be cooked as porridge. Various parts are used for medicinal and magical purposes. Commonly cultivated in garden ponds. *N. lotus* is the only other water lily native to the region; it has creamy white flowers.

**Limonium sinuatum*
E Statice **A** Papierblom

Plumbaginaceae
Spring–Autumn

Erect, bushy, short-lived perennial up to 400mm high; occurring on disturbed sites in fynbos, renosterveld and karroid shrubland, especially along roadsides. Stems longitudinally winged. Leaves oblanceolate, deeply pinnately lobed, hairy. Flowers in showy clusters at the tips of branches; calyx funnel-shaped, dry and membranous, purple; petals white.

A native of the Mediterranean region. Popular in dried-flower arrangements because the flowers retain their form and colour for many months after gathering. Cultivars are available with calyces (sing. calyx) in shades of pink, red, orange, yellow, blue and lavender. *Limonium* is a genus of some 300 species of cosmopolitan distribution, especially Mediterranean; most are found on open seashores or salt marshes.

Plumbago auriculata

E Plumbago   **A** Kaapse bloublommetjie

Plumbaginaceae

Spring–Autumn

Scrambling, much-branched shrub, up to 2.5m high; occurring in thicket and bushveld, often in rocky places. Leaves oblong or wedge-shaped, lower surface sometimes with numerous tiny white spots (calcium salts excreted by glands); stalk short, slightly winged, with two small lobes ('ears') at the base. Flowers in terminal racemes; petals pale blue, each with a purple midrib; calyx with sticky hairs; anthers blue.

A popular garden ornamental worldwide; makes an excellent flowering hedge. White- and dark blue-flowered cultivars available. Effectively combined in gardens with the yellow-flowered form of *Tecomaria capensis* (page 66), which flowers at the same time. Various parts used in traditional medicine. *P. zeylanica* is a smaller plant with white flowers.

Conostomium natalense

E Wild pentas   **A** Wildepentas

Rubiaceae

Summer

Erect, herbaceous to slightly woody perennial shrublet, up to 1m high; occurring in grassland and associated bushveld, often on forest margins or in disturbed places. Leaves opposite, lanceolate, 30–75 × 6–25mm; midrib conspicuously sunken above; base ± rounded; stalk very short; stipules present, interpetiolar. Flowers in terminal heads, surrounded by leafy bracts; corolla tube up to 18mm long, pale blue or lilac, rarely white; calyx lobes long and narrow, persisting in fruit.

Conostomium has flowers with four petals, a useful character to distinguish it from members of *Pentanisia*, a rather similar-looking genus that has five petals. Parts of the plant are used by the Zulu in traditional medicine, whereas the roots are utilised as love charms and for magical purposes by the Venda.

Pentanisia prunelloides

E Hairy-leaved pentanisia **A** Sooibrandbossie

Rubiaceae
Spring–Summer

Herbaceous perennial shrublet, up to 0.5m high, with trailing to erect annual stems from a thick, tuberous rootstock; occurring in grassland. Leaves opposite, extremely variable in size, usually ± hairy. Flowers congested in dense terminal heads, pale to deep purplish blue.

The herbaceous nature of the above-ground parts belies the true age of the plants; judged from the great size of their underground tubers, many are estimated to be several decades old. Both the Afrikaans common name (meaning 'heartburn shrublet') and the Zulu/Xhosa name, *icishamlilo* (meaning 'that which puts out the fire') refer to the use of the plant to treat heartburn; a small piece of fresh root is chewed and swallowed. Tubers are also extensively used for various other ailments. *P. angustifolia* has ± hairless leaves.

Aptosimum procumbens (= *A. depressum*)

E Karoo violet **A** Karooviooltjie

Scrophulariaceae
Summer

Mat-forming perennial herb, up to 1.5m in diameter, which sprouts annually from a woody rootstock; occurring in grassland and karroid shrubland. Stems prostrate, radiating from the root, leafy throughout. Leaves narrowly or broadly obovate; stalk much shorter than the lamina. Flowers produced all along the stems, often in profusion, irregular, deep blue or violet, rarely maroon, with white markings at the throat.

Very attractive when in full bloom, otherwise a rather insignificant plant. Used medicinally for bladder and other ailments in man and for *krimpsiekte* in sheep. *A. spinescens*, with very similar flowers, is an erect, branched shrublet with needle-like, spine-tipped leaves that are densely crowded along the stems. It is confined to the Nama-Karoo and Succulent Karoo biomes.

Jamesbrittenia macrantha (= *Sutera macrantha*)   Scrophulariaceae
E Sekhukhune wild phlox   **A** Sekhukhune-wildefloks   Summer

Perennial shrublet, up to 1m high; occurring in bushveld and associated grassland, usually on soils rich in heavy metals derived from ultramafic rocks, often along roadsides. Leaves almost hairless, with a few scattered glistening glands; margin toothed. Flowers solitary in axils of upper leaves, which are reduced; corolla with lobes lilac to deep violet-mauve, throat yellowish green.

One of several plant species endemic to Sekhukhuneland. An attractive but relatively unknown plant similar to *J. grandiflora*, a species often cultivated and easily distinguished by its leaves, which are hairy and densely covered in glistening glands, particularly on the lower surface. It occurs from Mount Sheba to Barberton along the Drakensberg Escarpment, and in the Eastern Highlands of Swaziland.

Pseudoselago serrata (= *Selago serrata*)   Scrophulariaceae
E Cape blue haze   **A** Kaapse blouaarbos   Spring–Summer

Erect or sprawling, evergreen perennial shrublet, up to 1m high; occurring in fynbos, usually among rocks on mountain slopes. Stems stout, angular. Leaves densely arranged, oval, 5–10mm wide, thick and leathery, tips slightly recurved, hairless; margin distinctly toothed.

Flowers very small, blue or mauve; borne in dense, round-topped heads, up to 120mm in diameter at the ends of the stems. The individual units of the inflorescences elongate at fruiting time. This is the most showy member of the genus in the Western Cape; bought flowers may be used for arrangements. In cultivation it does best in the winter-rainfall area. *P. spuria* also has round-topped inflorescences (though often smaller) and clearly toothed leaves, but the latter are only 1–3mm wide.

JOHN MANNING

Tetraselago wilmsii (= *Selago wilmsii*)
E Blue haze **A** Blouaarbos

Scrophulariaceae
Summer–Autumn

Evergreen perennial shrublet, up to 0.5m high, with several erect, usually unbranched stems; occurring in grassland, usually in rocky places. Leaves ± 20 × 3–5mm. Flowers very small, blue, mauve or rarely white, densely arranged in small racemes of 10–14 flowers, the latter aggregated into terminal, slightly round-topped inflorescences up to ± 60mm in diameter.

In *T. nelsonii* the partial inflorescences are ± rounded heads. *T. natalensis* (KwaZulu-Natal) has the partial inflorescences more loosely arranged, each with 10–45 flowers, and the leaves are slightly longer (± 30 × 3mm). *Tetraselago* is superficially very similar to *Selago* and the two genera appear similar when in flower. However, the fruit in the former is a tiny dehiscent capsule, and in the latter, four indehiscent nutlets.

Walafrida geniculata (= *Selago geniculata*)
E Waterfinder **A** Persaarbos

Scrophulariaceae
Summer–Winter

Perennial shrublet, up to 0.5m high, old growth woody; occurring in karroid vegetation types, usually in low-lying parts. Leaves bright green, strap-shaped, up to 20 × 2mm; margin smooth. Flowers densely arranged in 50–100mm-long spikes at branch tips, lilac to purple, occasionally white, very small, each with two upward- and three downward-pointing petals.

Plants may be female (relatively rare) or bisexual (illustrated), the inflorescences of the latter being denser and somewhat rounder. Very palatable to livestock, drought-resistant and resprouts quickly after grazing, or even after light rain. Its presence is indicative of good veld condition. Easily confused with *Selago albida*, which is strongly scented, tends to have more rounded inflorescences and prefers rocky mountains and ridges.

BOSSIE KOTZÉ

Solanum campylacanthum
(= *S. delagoense*; *S. panduriforme*)
E Poison apple **A** Gifappel

Solanaceae
Spring–Summer

Perennial shrublet, up to 0.5m high, sprouting from an extensive system of underground stems; occurring in grassland and bushveld. Stems usually without prickles. Leaves lanceolate, both surfaces rather similar in colour; margin smooth. Flowers solitary or in small axillary clusters; petals mauve; anthers with very short filaments, cohering to form a central cone, bright yellow. Fruit round, ± 20mm in diameter, yellow.

A very variable species (this is subsp. *panduriforme*). The root and fruit are widely used in traditional medicine. Both the green and ripe fruit are poisonous. All native species of *Solanum* have anthers with minute pores at the tip. Bees release the pollen grains from the pores by rapid vibration of their thoracic muscles as they hang from the anther cone (so-called 'buzz pollination').

BRAAM VAN WYK & SASA MALAN

Xerophyta retinervis
E Monkey's tail **A** Bobbejaanstert

Velloziaceae
Spring

A deciduous perennial, with stout, erect, sometimes sparsely branched stems; occurring on rocky ridges in grassland and bushveld. Stems densely covered with a thick mantle of fire-charred, closely packed, persistent leaf bases, and have numerous densely packed roots (stem tissue dies off at an early stage) inside. Leaves grass-like, keeled, in terminal tufts. Flowers deep to pale mauve or white, borne in abundance on slender stalks among the leaves, especially after fire.

The persistent leaf bases provide excellent protection against veld fires. Plants are very slow-growing and large ones are estimated to be well over 100 years old. Attempts to grow these interesting plants in gardens have failed. The root is used in traditional medicine to treat asthma.

Verbena aristigera (= *V. tenuisecta*)

E Fine-leaved verbena **A** Fynblaarverbena

Verbenaceae
Spring–Summer

Short-lived, sprawling herb, up to 200mm high; occurring in disturbed places, particularly along roadsides. Leaves deeply dissected, both surfaces hairy; base stem-clasping. Flowers in dense, flat-topped, terminal spikes, the latter elongating considerably as new flowers are produced at the ends; petals bright mauve, fading to blue, occasionally white, tips distinctly notched.

A native of South America; widely grown as a ground cover in gardens. Naturalised throughout the region, but not a serious weed of cultivation, and control measures are rarely required. *Verbena*, a genus of ± 200 species, is mostly confined to the tropical and temperate parts of North and South America, with a few in Europe and Asia; there are no species native to South Africa. Many species are used in traditional medicine.

Verbena bonariensis

E Wild verbena **A** Blouwaterbossie

Verbenaceae
Summer

Erect, sparsely branched annual, up to 2m high, with rough hairs; occurring in grassland and disturbed sites, especially in wet places. Stems tough and fibrous. Leaves opposite, stalkless and ± clasping at the base. Flowers in branched, flat-topped, congested inflorescences, very small, purple.

A native of South America. The flowers are popular with butterflies and other insects. Inflorescences are dried, coloured and used in dried-flower arrangements. *V. brasiliensis* (from South America) has leaves that are distinctly stalked with the base narrowly tapering; its inflorescences tend to be slender and smaller. *V. officinalis* (from Europe), a smaller plant, has ± well-spaced flowers on long, narrow, terminal spikes, and lower leaves that are deeply lobed or pinnately divided.

Asclepias albens (= A. affinis)

E Cartwheels **A** Wawielmelkbos

Asclepiadaceae

Summer

Perennial herb with a tuberous rootstock; occurring in grassland. Most parts with milky latex. Leaves ovate, with coarse hairs. Flowers distinctly stalked, clustered into a terminal, flat-topped head, which is turned sideways; corolla lobes reflex, white, greenish or cream, often tinged with pink; corona lobes ± square, opening upward, green or yellowish.

Flowers (see page 142) highly specialised. Stamens and style are fused together to form a central column. Five greenish cups (corona) secrete nectar. Pollen grains united into pollinia and connected in pairs (five per flower) to a wishbone-shaped structure, all concealed except for a tiny blackish gland. Pollinia are withdrawn when the legs or mouthparts of visiting insects are guided toward the gland by special grooves on the column.

Pachycarpus campanulatus

E Fairy-bell pachycarpus **A** Feeklokkie-pachycarpus

Asclepiadaceae

Summer

Slender, erect perennial herb, up to 600mm high, sprouting annually from a tuber; occurring in grassland. Most parts with milky latex. Stems one or two, ± coarse haired. Leaves opposite, erect, spreading, very narrowly linear to lanceolate, 64–165 × 2–10mm; margin rolled downward. Flowers in a terminal umbel with 3–14 flowers, usually drooping; corolla cup- or bell-shaped, 10–15mm long, pale green or dull cream-green, becoming cream-brown in old flowers.

Plants flower most profusely in regularly burned grassland. The generic name is derived from the Greek, *pachys* (= thick) and *carpus* (= fruit), referring to the large, inflated fruit of some of the species (not this one). At least 24 species are known from the region, all confined to summer-rainfall grassland.

MARTIN VON FINTEL

Erica sessiliflora
E Green heath **A** Groenheide

Ericaceae
Autumn–Spring

Erect, robust evergreen shrub, up to 2m high; occurring in fynbos, usually in marshy areas, or between rocks where there is an increase in water runoff. Stems densely covered in leaves, hairless. Leaves needle-like, 4–14mm long. Flowers tightly arranged in spikes near the ends of branches; corolla tubular, 16–30mm long, pale green; anthers not protruding; sepals fleshy.

Easy to identify, even if not in flower. The fleshy sepals are persistent and increase in size during fruiting. They acquire a reddish tinge and, together with the fruit, may remain on the plant for many years. Fruiting heads reminiscent of a cancerous deformity or a fungal infection; responsible for the Afrikaans name *mielieheide*, because it resembles a maize cob. Persistent fruits release their seeds only after fire, a trait known as serotiny.

Eucomis autumnalis
E Common pineapple flower **A** Gewone wildepynappel

Hyacinthaceae
Summer

Deciduous herb with a bulb; occurring in grassland, especially in moist places or on rocky ridges. Leaves in a basal rosette, strap-shaped, 150–550 × 40–130mm, hairless, often with a wavy margin. Inflorescence stalk erect, ending in a tuft of green leaf-like bracts above the densely packed flowers; tepals pale yellow-green to whitish.

The inflorescence has the appearance of a pineapple, hence the common names. The bulbs are extensively used in traditional medicine to treat a variety of ailments, including urinary-tract and lung diseases, stomach ache, fevers, biliousness, blood disorders and venereal diseases. Over-collecting for the herbal trade is a serious threat to natural populations of this species. A genus of at least 10 species, all confined to southern Africa.

GLOSSARY

Synonyms are supplied for some terms, and are given in brackets at the end of the definition. Also see the line drawings on pages 142 and 143.

Annual a plant that completes its life cycle from germination to seeding and death within one year.

apical pore a tiny opening at the tip of the pollen-bearing anther.

appressed lying close to or pressed flat against a surface or structure, as the hairs on certain leaves.

berry a many-seeded fleshy fruit with a soft outer portion and the seeds embedded in the fleshy or pulpy tissue (e.g. the tomato).

biennial a plant that grows and develops in the first year, and fruits and seeds in the second; living for two growing seasons.

bract a usually small leaf-like structure, in the axil of which arises a flower or a branch of an inflorescence.

bulb a swollen underground organ comprising a short disc-like stem with fleshy and tightly overlapping leaf bases (e.g. the onion).

capsule a dry fruit produced by an ovary comprising two or more united carpels and usually opening by slits or pores.

corm a shortened (compressed) and swollen underground stem that produces leaves at the top, enclosed by dry fibrous leaf bases; characteristic of many Iridaceae.

deciduous shedding leaves at the end of the growing season.

dehiscent opening when mature, as in anthers or fruit. A 'valve' is one of the parts produced when a capsule or pod dehisces.

discoid having only disc florets (e.g. some members of Asteraceae).

dissected deeply divided or irregularly cut into many segments.

distal toward the tip, or the end, of an organ (e.g. root, stem or leaf).

enantiomorphy showing 'handedness'; with structures (e.g. keel, style, stamens) twisted or bent toward either the left or the right.

enantiostyly a phenomenon in which the style is bent to the right in some flowers (or plants) and to the left in other flowers (or plants); flowers show 'handedness'.

endemic strictly confined to a specific region or substrate.

epiphyte a plant that grows on another plant but is not parasitic on it.

evergreen retaining green leaves throughout the year, even during winter months.

exserted projecting beyond surrounding parts, as stamens protruding from a corolla; not included.

fallow said of land left uncultivated after being ploughed and seeded at an earlier time.

-fid (two-fid) dividing into two lobes or parts.

floriferous bearing many flowers.

flower head a dense inflorescence of many small, crowded, often stalkless flowers (florets) at the end of a common stalk; ± spherical or dish-shaped.

globose spherical, rounded.

forb a non-grassy herbaceous plant.

hemiparasite a parasitic plant that contains chlorophyll and is therefore partly self-sustaining, as in many Orobanchaceae. Holoparasites by comparison lack chlorophyll and are entirely dependent on the host for nourishment.

herb (herbaceous) a plant that does not develop persistent woody tissue above ground and either dies at the end of the growing season or overwinters by means of underground organs (e.g. rhizomes, bulbs, corms).

heterostylous with styles of different lengths in flowers of plants in the same species.

incised with the margin deeply cut.

indigenous a plant occurring naturally in an area and not introduced from elsewhere (= native).

inflorescence any arrangement of more than one flower; the flowering portion of a plant, e.g. head, spike, panicle, raceme.

interpetiolar between the leaf stalks, as an interpetiolar stipule that extends from the base of one leaf stalk across the stem to the base of the stalk of the opposite leaf (e.g. in many Rubiaceae).

involucre a whorl of bracts subtending a flower or flower cluster.

karroid Karoo-like; used to describe vegetation types typical or reminiscent of the semidesert Karoo region of South Africa, namely a sparse vegetation dominated by dwarf perennial shrublets.

lax spread out and drooping; usually growing close to the ground.

lobe a part or segment of an organ (e.g. leaf, petal) that is deeply divided from the rest of the organ but not separated.

locule a chamber or cavity in the ovary containing one or more ovules or seeds.

midrib the central or largest vein or rib of a leaf or other organ.

naturalised an alien plant, introduced from a foreign into a new area, where it has become established and is reproducing successfully.

nectary any structure that produces nectar, such as glands or special glandular hairs.

nutlet a small, dry, single-seeded and indehiscent fruit with a hard outer covering.

panicle a branched inflorescence with an axis that can continue to grow and does not end in a flower (i.e. the axis is indeterminate). Each branch bears two or more flowers.

papilla (plural: papillae) a soft nipple-shaped protuberance.

pappus hairs, bristles or scales that replace the calyx in some members of the Asteraceae; they often facilitate fruit dispersal.

peltate shield-shaped; a flat structure borne on a stalk attached to the lower surface rather than to the base or margin.

perennial a plant living for three or more years.

persistent remaining attached and not falling off.

pioneer describes the first plant species that colonise bare or disturbed areas.

pod a general term applied to any dry and many-seeded dehiscent fruit, formed from one unit or carpel.

pollination the transfer of pollen from the anther to the stigma.

pollinium (plural: pollinia) a mass of coherent pollen grains transported as a single unit during pollination, as in members of the Asclepiadaceae and Orchidaceae.

prostrate with stems trailing or lying flat on the ground, but not rooting (= procumbent).

raceme an inflorescence in which the flowers are borne consecutively along a single (unbranched) axis, the lowest on the axis being the oldest. Each flower has a stalk.

radiate describing flower heads in some Asteraceae, which have ray florets on the outside and disc florets on the inside. (See also page 142.)

reflexed bent abruptly downward or backward.

rhizome a creeping (± horizontal) underground stem that sends up new stems and leaves each season.

rosette an arrangement of leaves radiating from a crown or centre, usually at ground level.

scales any thin, flat, often membranous structure.

scalloped the margin notched with rounded or broad and blunt teeth or projections (= crenate, crenulate).

shrub a perennial woody plant less than 2m high with usually two or more stems arising from or near the ground; differs from a tree in that it is smaller and does not possess a trunk or bole.

shrublet a low-growing perennial with stems that are woody mainly towards the base; usually less than 1m high, and often ± prostrate (= subshrub, undershrub).

simple leaf with only a single blade.

spadix a spike with small flowers crowded on a thickened axis.

spathe a large bract that is sometimes leaf- or petal-like and encloses the young flower or inflorescence.

spike an inflorescence with stalkless flowers arranged along an elongated unbranched axis.

spine a hard sharply pointed structure, often long and narrow. Usually a modified leaf or stipule.

spur a tubular or sac-like projection of a flower, as from the base of a petal or sepal; it usually contains nectar-secreting glands.

sub-climax describes vegetation at a stage prior to the attainment of a fully mature, stable (climax) vegetation community.

taxon a group, unit, or rank of classification, for example, a species, a genus or a family.

tendril a slender, usually coiling part of the leaf or stem that serves to support the stem; a climbing organ.

tepals in this book, used for the parts (segments) of a perianth that are not, or are scarcely, differentiated into calyx and corolla; segments either sepal- or petal-like (= perianth segments).

terminal at the tip (= apical, or at the distal end).

tuber an underground swollen part of a stem or root, which stores food; capable of producing new shoots from buds on its surface.

tubercles a small tuber-like swelling or projection.

ultramafic rocks volcanic rocks that give rise to soils with a high magnesium to calcium ratio and high concentrations of toxic heavy metals.

umbel an umbrella-shaped inflorescence in which the flower stalks all arise from the top of the main stem.

undulate with a wavy margin.

venation the pattern of veining on a leaf blade.

weed an aggressive, problem plant that usually colonises disturbed habitats and cultivated lands.

wing any thin flat extension of an organ, as in winged fruit or seed.

Parts of a flower

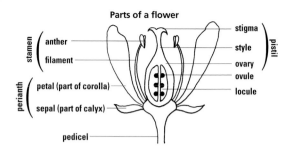

- stamen
  - anther
  - filament
- perianth
  - petal (part of corolla)
  - sepal (part of calyx)
- pistil
  - stigma
  - style
  - ovary
  - ovule
  - locule
- pedicel

Asclepiadaceae (milkweed family) flower

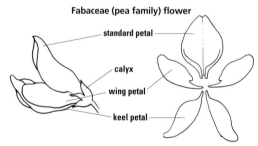

- corona lobes
- site of pollinia pair (concealed)
- petals

Pollinia pair (enlarged)

- gland (corpusculum)
- translator arm
- pollinium

Fabaceae (pea family) flower

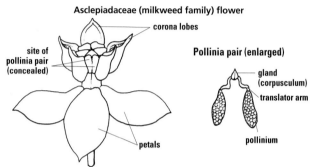

- standard petal
- calyx
- wing petal
- keel petal

Asteraceae (daisy family) radiate flower head

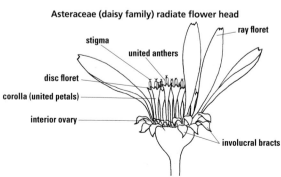

- ray floret
- stigma
- united anthers
- disc floret
- corolla (united petals)
- interior ovary
- involucral bracts

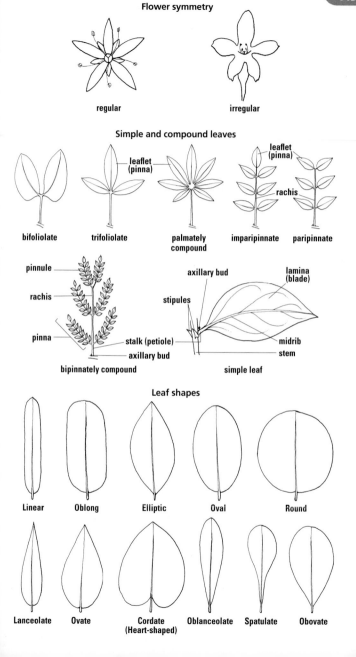

Flower symmetry

regular

irregular

Simple and compound leaves

bifoliolate

trifoliolate

leaflet (pinna)

palmately compound

imparipinnate

paripinnate

leaflet (pinna)

rachis

pinnule

rachis

pinna

stalk (petiole)

axillary bud

bipinnately compound

axillary bud

stipules

lamina (blade)

midrib

stem

simple leaf

Leaf shapes

Linear

Oblong

Elliptic

Oval

Round

Lanceolate

Ovate

Cordate (Heart-shaped)

Oblanceolate

Spatulate

Obovate

FURTHER READING

Le Roux, P.M., Kotze, C.D. & Nel, G.P. 1994. *Bossieveld: Grazing Plants of the Karoo and Karoo-like areas.* Department of Agriculture & National Botanical Institute, Pretoria.

Manning, J. 2007. *Field Guide to Fynbos.* Struik Nature, Cape Town.

Manning, J. 2010. *Field Guide to Wild Flowers of South Africa.* Struik Nature, Cape Town.

Pooley, E. 1998. *A Field Guide to Wild Flowers: KwaZulu-Natal and the Eastern Region.* Natal Flora Publications Trust, Durban.

Pooley, E. 2003. *Mountain Flowers: a Field Guide to the Flora of the Drakensberg and Lesotho.* Natal Flora Publications Trust, Durban.

South African Wild Flower Guides, by various authors. **1:** Namaqualand; **2:** Outeniqua, Tsitsikamma & Eastern Little Karoo; **3:** Cape Peninsula; **4:** Transvaal Lowveld & Escarpment; **5:** Hottentots Holland to Hermanus; **6:** Karoo; **7:** West Coast; **8:** Southern Overberg; **9:** Nieuwoudtville, Bokkeveld Plateau and Hantam; **10:** Cederberg, Clanwilliam & Biedouw Valley; **11:** Eastern Cape; **12:** Table Mountain National Park. Botanical Society of South Africa, Claremont.

Van Wyk, B. & Malan, S. 1997. *Field Guide to the Wild Flowers of the Highveld*, Struik Publishers, Cape Town.

Vlok, J. & Schutte-Vlok, A. 2010. *Plants of the Klein Karoo.* Umdaus Press, Hatfield.

Oscularia deltoides; *a vygie from sandstone rocks in the Cape mountains.*

INDEX TO SCIENTIFIC NAMES

Synonyms are followed by a ♦ sign. Species listed in a lighter font are mentioned in the text, but are not treated in full.

INDEX TO AFRIKAANS COMMON NAMES

INDEX TO ENGLISH COMMON NAMES

Nemesia versicolor *is an annual spring-flowering herb from the Cape and Namaqualand.*